Y
WE
STAR HERE

THE GREAT BOOK OF WHOLISTIC WEALTH SECRETS

What You Must Be and Do

to Start Your Wealth Journey

By

Martin Godfrey Legido

ISBN: 978-1-9993497-1-4

DEDICATION

I would like to dedicate this book to my close and extended family for the love and support over the years... Ana, Jill, Jan, Dasha & Arty, Kristiana & Luca, Tomas & Tommy, Teresa, Josep Legido & family, Brian & Han... and so many more, thank you all.

To Ray
& Family
Best Wishes
for everything
Martin
Feb 2019.

ACKNOWLEDGMENTS

To quote Stephen R Covey (a guiding light on my personal journey): "Interdependence is a higher value than independence."

I believe we learn something every day, and often from those we meet and interact with, and I would like to acknowledge the following:

- To mother Josefina and father Bill and, for supporting me as a child and young adult to have the confidence to make my way in the world, become qualified as an accountant and take some high flying jobs.

- To sister Jill in Paris, for supporting and loving and of course at times, antagonising! But always lovingly.

- To Cousins John Bull and Frances and their kids Luli, Michael and Catherine, and of course Aunt Carmen and Uncle John for supporting as extended family.

- To Ex wife Teresa Godfrey for, again supporting me through thick and thin and having those two pesky kids Jan and Kristiana!

- Charles Young of New York, for showing the ropes at senior level in the corporate world in USA and internationally. My first true mentor, thanks Charlie.

- George F Metcalfe – my Life Coach for almost 20 years... thanks George for sharing your abundant knowledge and experience on this planet.

- Gill Fielding for being one of the first in the UK to promote and teach Wealth Education, for property and more... ground breaking at the time and continues to be so.

- Iain Edwards of Elite Legacy (Rich Dad Education etc) for directing this organisation and helping me (and thousands more) to generate wealth and financial stability.

- Nigel Washington – Vicar at St Mary Magdalene Church in Bedfordshire, a truly spiritual guy and friend... thanks for the guidance

- Xue Si Qi, Master of Qi Gong and Yi Quan in Beijing for teaching me over the years how to defend myself (ouch!) but also to give great healing.

- Jan Voormeij, my first serious teacher of martial arts in Amsterdam, still a friend and teacher. Bedankt Jan.

And many many more who've helped along the way.

Martin has opened my eyes to the development world, and as such has me negotiating a £6m project much sooner than I thought I could be. This is just one of the many lessons I have taken away from this as his business knowledge spans so wide.

He's a great person to have spent time learning from and I can't recommend him enough to anyone looking to get out of their own way and move up to the next level in their career.

- James E.

***

We completed a mentorship in UK with Martin Godfrey. His knowledge and experience was excellent, and he tailored the sessions to our requirements. He went above and beyond our expectations with his holistic business viewpoints which went beyond the property industry. He remained realistic throughout which was essential.

- Ali K.

***

Thanks for all your support these past 3 days in our mentorship. Now we feel we are much better prepared to move forward with our goals.

- Eliane R.

***

I have just completed a 3-day mentorship with Martin Godfrey. I feel very privileged to have learned from Martin who has had over 25 years of property and business investment experience. His advice will provide a solid foundation for my journey for many years to come.

Martin is a friendly, down-to-earth, experienced mentor. He is direct but courteous at the same time. Martin is always willing to provide answers to my questions. He is energetic, and keeps our conversations engaging during the mentorship. I feel very privileged to have learned from Martin. His advice will set a solid foundation for my business and property journey. Martin goes above and beyond to share his experience with me and answers all my questions. He directs me to the strategies I should focus on now and in the near future.

- Helen L.

***

Martin is the best Mentor we could imagine to have. He understood well our circumstances and he made sure that the Mentorship is fit for purpose. He shared with us his experience and gave very good advice regarding our business and its future. He was always open for a discussion and was happy to answer any question we had. He made us to become more confident, motivated. These 3 days were very transformational and life changing. Thank you Martin for everything!

- Nadime S.

***

Martin Godfrey Legido was an amazing mentor. Along with being highly knowledgeable in property specifically, he is also extremely clever in business and has shown us how to expand and scale our property ventures on a corporate level. What was a few hundred thousand pound plan is now a multi-million plan.

- Ray S.

CONTENTS

CHAPTER 1

What's This Book All About?

Firstly, a warning! If you earn over £50k ($70k) and you have assets of more than £1M ($1.4), put this book down immediately! It's not for you! It's for those aspiring to make that money or more… Yes, hmmmm, but maybe you could still pick up a tip or two…

Wealth really is a strange thing. It seems to accumulate with some and not with others. I think it clearly has a lot to do with the things we do in our lives and the actions we take, the thoughts that we have. But sometimes wealth, good energy, comes in a form of flow that seems to accrue with some people and not with others.

It's a subject that has interested me for most of my adult life. On a personal level, how do you attain wealth? How do you accumulate it? How can you keep it? But equally I am intrigued by the causes of wealth, the circumstances under which wealth is generated, created.

But as someone who has managed to become wealthy, I can honestly say I have done so and continue to do so in an ethical manner. That to me is very important, because I don't view the accumulation of wealth as a sign of greed. Some might see it that way, but to me wealth isn't just about money; it's about well-being too. You can be wealthy financially but also wealthy within yourself, a wealth of health if you like, in mind and body. That is in essence what I aspire to achieve on a personal level.

I think most of us, the vast majority of us, live our lives in a righteous way. There are ethics in society and we want to live by those ethics. Of course there's a fringe element, there are people who have made tremendous wealth in unscrupulous ways and illegal activities, drugs and crime mainly, and financial fraud to a certain extent. But the nature of crime has changed a lot – you don't get so many people robbing banks these days, a lot of it is going on digitally. But I'll leave that to the law enforcement agencies and CID!

Essentially, I believe most of us want to become financially independent and financially free and that is what this book is all about – giving you the guidance to achieve that position.

The term "financially free" has been bandied about a huge amount and to be honest I'm not too keen on it. What do we mean by it? What do we mean by financially free, financially independent?

Well I think that is quite a personal thing and will mean different things to different people.

If you are an Arab prince in Saudi Arabia financial freedom is probably an income of £1 million a year. For people living in London, maybe an income of £3,000 a month without actually having to present yourself at a place of work, an office, factory, retail outlet or civil service – £3,000 a month would probably do the job.

But achieving an income of that amount without actually having to go to work for it is probably not within the bounds of most people reading this.

Or so you may think.

You may well say I am writing this from Cloud Cuckoo Land, and I can understand that, a little bit. But the thing is, the truth of the matter is, anyone can become financially independent – if they use some common sense and make the use of all the opportunities that are right there under their noses.

How can I can be so brazen as to suggest such a thing?

That's easy – because I have done exactly what I was shown to do by others and have managed to carve out my own niche to become financially free.

The hardest part was deciding to do it. Once you make that decision and get on that road, everything begins to open up to you. The key is realising you have to start somewhere and actually make that move.

So, ***your wealth starts here,*** and I am going to take you all the way from the very basics of common sense money-management right through to wealth creation and consolidation and a lot more besides. Think of it as your very own blueprint for financial freedom.

This book then is all about wealth – or to be more specific – *your wealth* and includes methods and techniques you should know and grasp in order to keep more of what you have and also to create more wealth for yourself.

Importantly though, we also want to encourage you to have a deep look at yourself because personal development is crucial if you are going to succeed with keeping what you have and making more for yourself so you can become financially free.

So –

- ✓ **Personal Development**
- ✓ **Keeping Your Wealth**
- ✓ **Creating More Wealth**

These are the three key elements and they are all really interlinked, you can't really do one without the other, as you will see.

It's what I like to call a *"WHOLISTIC" approach.*

In other words, we're going to be looking at you, how you need to be in good health and be feeding the mind, following a healthy diet and exercising, in order to be able to pay proper attention to the money you have coming in, your income and what you do with it.

With your income we're going to explore the various factors that help you keep more of what you have, we're going to look at defensive strategies, we're going to look at what you've already got, how you keep it, how you don't just waste it. How maybe you need to measure it and control what you're spending, how you focus on spending on things you really want to spend on, things you really, really love and not just things that you need to spend on.

Obviously there's a whole load of stuff – rent or mortgage, utility bills and so on that you're going to have to spend on, but there's invariably a percentage which you can choose with discretion what you want to spend on.

Some of you reading this will, I am sure, not actually be able to enjoy a discretionary spend because you don't make enough on a monthly basis to cover your outgoings, and so you're in deficit every month and are using credit cards and so forth to cover your basic needs.

So we're going to look at:

DEFENSIVE STRATEGIES

This is where we look at how to keep what you've got. We're going to look at banks, we're going to look at credit cards and all this is really basic stuff, but hey, you know, we need to be reminded of basic stuff! I certainly do. If I say, "Do you know this, that and the other?" you'll probably say, "I know it…" But do you **do** it? Often you don't.

For example, let me ask you, do you keep a budget of your monthly, annual, weekly expenditure? If you do not, then I say to you – you really should be. It's a basic, easy technique to adopt to help you keep more of what you've got. Very basic.

So what you should be looking at is keeping what you've got (it is actually a way of creating more, as I'll explain later) and not being ripped off by financial institutions. We know that the banks are out there essentially to make as much money as they can out of us. We know that bankers are programmed to do that, even the high street banks, and of course we are bombarded with massive amounts of publicity saying what good guys they are and how they are doing everything in our interest and so forth, but, well… hmmm… You've only got to speak to somebody who has worked for one of the large banks, you know, they're offering a service, depending on the bank, and you may find it's a reasonable cost. I tend to think not, but there you go.

Credit cards. I am sure you must have one. Maybe you have more than one, perhaps even as many as five; you'd be surprised how many people have five or more. You will find the credit card industry has blossomed in the last 30 years. The amount of credit we have, I don't know how many trillions of pounds it is at the moment, but it is quite staggering. Yet we have very short memories. There was the financial crash a mere nine years ago. Before that there was a financial crash a mere 10 years ago. And so on back. There was one in the 80s. One in the 70s and so on. People have very short memories but that doesn't stop them going out and spending like mad.

So we're going to look at the defensive things that you can implement, and there are things you can start today, right now, there are things you can start first thing tomorrow morning, simple things that you can pick up from reading this book and using the resources it contains.

And then we're going to look at:

OFFENSIVE STRATEGIES

How do you make more money? Are you in a job? If you are in a job what can we do to get you to earn more? How can you please your employer so that they are prepared to pay you more?

If you're not in a job but in business, what things can be done to improve your turnover and profit? Obviously this is a deep, deep subject but we're going to go in deep and give you the nuts and bolts which will hopefully ignite some sparks, that's the general idea here. I am hoping to ignite some sparks so that you go away with ideas you can take further forward and if you want to get in touch with me to talk anything over, that is fine, I am happy for you to do that, and you can do that by using any of the contact details at the end of this book.

So if you're in business, we will be showing you some methods to improve the performance of your enterprise. If you're not in business then you might want to consider starting one and we'll be talking about that in more detail. Then we'll be looking at other asset classes of investment such as property, wine and art and other investment opportunities. As you may know, I am a property investment mentor and have been a business mentor for a major UK and American training organisation. And I'm pleased to say that we normally do a really good job for the students and I am delighted, not in any egotistical way, that I am able to make a real difference to people's lives and that's why I am doing this, writing this book, generating education, propagating our concept **The Wealth Tree**, keeping it up to date and informative.

Of course I get paid for my time when mentoring and coaching and I do a certain amount of charitable work, but essentially I am doing this because I know I can make a difference to people's lives, improve their lives, help them to be able to enjoy financial independence so they can spend more time with their family or do more travelling or above all help them to be able to do more to help others.

AND THAT IS WHAT BEING FINANCIALLY FREE AND INDEPENDENT ALLOWS YOU - MORE TIME TO DO LESS WORK.

When you become financially independent you can relax a little bit. Maybe you can do some more work at the local church or mosque to help your fellow man. Maybe you can donate more to charities. Maybe you can take some time to go out to Africa or South America and help in developing countries. This is what financial independence can do for people. And for me personally, my mission is to help create financial freedom and independence for the many, not just the few.

To be honest, I get quite choked up by how many people are suffering in the UK at the moment. It pains me to read about all the food banks we now have across the country. Over 600 food banks, when only a few years ago we had none. What does that say about our society? Frankly, I think it's appalling.

POVERTY

When one looks at wealth across the world, it's quite alarming just how much poverty there is. The United Nations Millennium Development target was to halve world poverty from 1990 to 2015. This was actually achieved by 2010 which is great news, of course. But still, as of now, 17% of the population – which is 1.2 billion people – live below the $1.25 per day poverty benchmark and that has recently been revised to $1.09 a day. I guess it's global inflation. But it's still a lot of people living below the poverty line.

There are a lot of people dying out there from not having access to basic food or medication they need. And you'd be surprised, that's not just in developing countries, some of that is happening in very well developed countries in places such as the United States. Believe it or not we've got 33% – that's 2.2 billion people – living on less than $2 per day.

So I think, we've got to start somewhere to stop this happening and we're starting here and we're starting by writing this book to make people aware of the situation.

105 million people live in chronic hunger. Have you ever been hungry? When I was a kid growing up in London, I can't remember chronic hunger at all, but back in the day my mother used to say to us if you're still hungry at the end of the meal you can "fill up" on bread and butter. So, you know, food wasn't that abundant in my own childhood.

Three billion people are still cooking on open fires. Obviously that creates deforestation, pollution, and the general poverty creates ill health and the open fires are contributing to climate change.

The UK is the fifth largest and wealthiest economy in the world. The United States, Japan, China, and Germany are the top four. And then we vie for fifth and sixth place with France. So let's say we're a bit wealthier than the French in fifth. We've got 66 million people here in the UK and last year, 2017, the population grew by almost half a million (400,000). Much of that was down to immigration of course. It is predicted to be 72 million in 15 years.

The average UK net income after housing and tax is £359.00 per week, or about £18,000 per annum. The actual average gross income in the UK is £27,000 per annum and that's very much an average because you only have to go north of Watford, north of Birmingham and you will find much lower wages.

A poor household is considered to earn 60% of this or less, in other words about £200 per week, or £11,000 per annum. That's a poor household here in the UK. So "according to national statistics" 13 million people out of the 64 million do not have enough to live on. That is 20% of the UK population. Did you know that? It's shocking, isn't it? 20% don't have enough to live on and many have to rely on foodbanks to survive. Child poverty within that general poverty figure affects 25-50% of households in certain areas which is a quite alarming statistic to me.

But it's not just confined to the north, that is the thing. If I said to you Middlesbrough, you probably have a hunch it's a fairly downbeat, downtrodden area. It had steel works near there once upon a time and was thriving, but now there is a lot of poverty there. Yet, if you look in London, Tower Hamlets, even Westminster, there is child poverty in those areas too and these are all from government statistics.

Places like Pendle, Thanet in Kent, Bristol and various parts of the UK, poverty is all around us.

THE PAY GAP

Now approximately 91% of UK taxpayers earn less than £50,000. That shocked me when I first heard it, but I have known that for some time so I'm not too shocked by it now, but you know that is only 9% who are earning more than £50,000 and that £50,000 gross is going to be around £36,000 after tax and national insurance, so that is probably a financial figure for many, many people I would say – but it isn't a huge amount in truth. It's all relative, of course, £36k will be a lot to someone on just £10k and so on. But in today's high-cost world, those on £36k are not doing as well compared to say, a decade ago.

But if you're earning over £70,000, well, congratulations – you're in the top 4% of earners. And as you know there are a growing number of multi-millionaires and a growing number of billionaires in the world.

Just over ten years ago, to be on *The Sunday Times Rich List* you needed to be earning a minimum amount of £30 million, this was 2005. 2015 and it's £100 million. I mean it's tripled in ten years and we have had a financial crash in the middle of that. How did that happen? I'm not too sure.

So we think of £50-70 grand and we probably know all sorts of people earning those sorts of figures, but they are very much in the top sector of the UK economy.

It's a tough world out there and it is only going to get tougher. Becoming independently wealthy is going to become more crucial in the years to come, not only for your own daily hand-to-mouth survival, but for the things you want to do in life and then the "autumn years" when you have retired but still need an income to support you.

When you factor in all the changes the current Conservative government are trying to implement, things affecting the NHS, and creating a framework where people will have to put money into their own sick pay fund, you can see a time where we are all going to have to be self-sufficient and look after ourselves.

The exponential growth in the digital economy means that many of your jobs in retail, manufacturing, distribution etc. are going to disappear or change radically, another reason for writing this book… you will need to control assets to survive !

There has never been a more urgent need to start becoming financially independent. The purpose of this book is to help you find your way to that all-important financial freedom.

THE WHY… CONTINUED

My idea in writing this book is to help people!

I want to create ***lightbulb*** moments for the masses of people out there who are struggling and sometimes not struggling, just searching for to find their financial security.

We live in a time of massive change equivalent to the industrial revolution in the 19th century and this digital revolution is exponential!

It is revolutionary! It is exciting! But… it can be exclusive to whole sections of society and this is what is happening. Whilst we are creating more billionaires in the Western world we are also experiencing poverty on an increasing scale… more billionaires and more food banks!

The knowledge gap between those that have "cracked the code", and those who have not is most marked. In my mentoring and teachings I work with clients who are struggling with many business and investment issues… the cold hard facts are that many of the jobs currently around at the moment will ***not be there in 10 to 20 years!***

Only those that are marshalling resources and assets will be secure and this is the intention of this book! Certain kinds of jobs have not been sufficient for security for 20 years and are becoming much less so. At least 20 years ago the jobs were still there; now they are disappearing and changing fast!

SO WHAT IS TO BE DONE?

FIRSTLY ONE MUST:

- ✓ Study and understand what is happening out there
- ✓ Realise the consequences
- ✓ Study the various options and of course take action!

CHAPTER 2

The 7 Pillars of Wealth Wisdom

"Star performers start with a well-defined and concrete "impossible" goal they care deeply about and then they build a through-line that clearly connects here with there."

– *Robert K Cooper*

Again, none of what I am going to be discussing now is particularly new – it's variations on a theme, as it were. Because that is what happens through time, some of the philosophical and business ideas that have come up through the ages, many of them are simply re-worked versions of old texts and concepts, stemming from as far back as the ancient Greeks. These days it's called "putting a new spin on it". And there's nothing wrong with that whatsoever. Much of it is about how you say things, how you get them across. To be honest, I find some texts hard to fathom and follow. It's not necessarily the fault of the author, rather how we individually process information. That's why the "Books for Dummies" series has been so popular as they make complex ideas easier to follow for the layperson.

So essentially, I hope you are enjoying ***The Great Book of Wealth Secrets*** and the simplicity of the words. Again, not to brag about it, but many of my mentees have often remarked on how easily I can make things understood and for that I am thankful; it's nice to be appreciated!

So…

THE 7 PILLARS OF WEALTH WISDOM

If you want to be wealthy along with an abundant and happy life, you could have an abundant and happy life and become a monk and live in a cave, you don't need to be wealthy, but if you want to combine that with wealth, you absolutely need to be aware of the following things.

And in seminars and talks and mentoring that I've done, I find a lot of people are not aware of these. So we are going to start by being focused on seven; there could be more, it depends on how you measure them:

1. Multiple streams of income

Again studying multi-millionaires, they will typically have multiple streams of income, they don't depend on one. Looking at Richard Branson, I don't like to focus too much on him because he's really high profile, but there are loads of other wealthy individuals out there who do this one thing – they have many sources of income. So, as we seek to help you become financially free, take a note of the fact that *you must always look to get more than one stream of income.*

And typically that's going to mean being in business because if you're working and exchanging your time for money, something we strongly discourage, you're going to have limited opportunity for multiple streams of income.

Having said that, you might be a high-paid, high net-worth individual; you might be a barrister, a doctor, earning well and enjoying your profession, and why would you not? Therefore, you might be able to invest in stocks and shares, and invest in business as well. The point being you don't necessarily have to be in business, you can still be in a profession and earning well and still have multiple streams of income.

So, that is crucial and very important and many people don't understand that.

2. Understanding income and expenditure flows

One of the reasons I do this is because I have learned all about income and expenditure flows. And they are important to understand. I come across dysfunctional folk in various parts of the country who don't understand interest rates, don't really understand how banks operate, are not online or don't have a bank account. We're talking about the bottom section of society who are often really good folk, they just haven't had any exposure to proper knowledge about financial instruments. So one of the main reasons for me doing this is to help these people get off their knees, socially and financially, because we know that if people are financially stable, like people in Switzerland, they don't have too much crime over there. People are financially stable, they live better, their lives are better.

Poverty creates crime, encourages the baser instincts in people. Some parts of overcrowded cities in Africa are going to be full of people trying to abuse you, rip you off, and so on and so forth. So many people don't understand how these things work, but you really do need to be able to understand flows of income. How to plan them. And your expenditure, very basic stuff, but still people don't know it. Cash flow; again, in my mentoring role, students have to fill out quite a large questionnaire and I would say 20% of people who fill them out, and it's very simple listing of your income, total income and your expenditure, total expenditure, they just can't do it right. This is on a monthly basis, net income over expenditure or the other way around. It's quite an eye-opener sometimes for me when I see how little people know of these things.

I am not blaming them for not knowing, don't get me wrong. It's just surprising as I would have thought more people would take care of the money better. What you have coming in against what you have going out – it's very basic stuff.

Also understand the difference between and asset and a liability… this, again, is quite simple, but many don't understand the difference. It's like a personal balance sheet really. Very, very simple stuff but people get it wrong. They put in a monthly income, let's say a salary wage, two thousand something and they put in £30,000 which is their savings in the income bracket and they put some expenses in their liabilities, which is monthly expense. So clearly people don't understand this because if you're going to make money you need to know how to control it.

3. Understand debt and interest rates

We have already alluded to this, but many people do not and that's why some of these pay-day loans and high-interest lenders like Wonga, now closed down, I notice on TV advertising they were forced and I think had been for some time, to put in the interest rate and I have noticed that with Wonga adverts it kept the real interest low profile to catch people out.

People use them and I can't believe how that industry has grown and how they have been allowed to grow. And to my eternal shame at one point I was with some business colleagues, more than one group actually, and we were planning to launch a business like that and I felt, no, wait a minute, and the guy I was intending to do it with turned out to be a crook, and he really was, a fraudulent type crook, a real scamster, and I didn't see through it.

But I pulled back and I am so glad I did. A good lesson to learn – and an important one certainly for anyone going into business, especially with "partners". You have to know everything about the person and the business idea itself. Know everything you can so you can be absolutely sure it is legitimate and that the person(s) you are going to associate with are legitimate too.

As for money-lending – you do not need to go down that route to make money. Leave that to the banks. It's bad stuff.

So understand debt and interest. Understand interest rates, compound interest. Take advantage of tax and government benefit. And if you're unemployed and you're on benefits you will be doing that, won't you? Because many people on benefits, you ask them what their national insurance number is, and I haven't the slightest idea what mine is, but if you ask many of those folk they will know their national insurance number because they use it all the time to claim benefits.

4. Optimise tax and government benefits

But even if you are a receiving a wage, understand what the benefits are to government funds. Duncan Bannatyne, I remember reading his book some years ago, he realised there were government grants or support to convert places into elderly residences. There was government money to support these ventures and he sat down and read the rules and understood them and acted accordingly. And so could you. For example, if you wanted to get into HMO shared multi-let property you need to read the rules, the national rules and the local rules, and follow them. You need to be able to understand what's out there and how it all works.

It's all part of the self-education I mentioned earlier. Do your research. Become an expert. Not only will it help with your business start-ups, but it will make you feel good too. Self-esteem rises when you become knowledgeable. But bear in mind, you can't go against government law, so there really isn't much point trying. You may want to bend a few rules or think you are being clever trying to take the system on – but really it's not worth the effort. Simply take advantage of what there is already in place. If you can't beat them, join them. Take advantage of that.

5. Systemise your business

Once you get into business it is very good practice to divide it into systems to maximise operations and efficiency. There are some famous books out there on this very subject. The main point is, you don't want to be running around doing things on an ad hoc basis. Large companies are very good at systemising. Just think of an organisation like B&Q or Marks & Spencer, they are large companies and their operations are all rigorously systemised. There are operational manuals, people have to do things a certain way. They can't have managers going round trying to explain everything to every single individual employee. They have to follow rules and they have to systemise it.

And I would encourage you to do very much the same with any business you start. That way it becomes more efficient, becomes more cost-effective, and again I'm not always, you know, bit like a doctor, do as I say not as I do, I don't always do this, I sometimes get a bit bored and don't do that. But that's what you should be doing. It saves time and energy in the long run and that is invaluable for any business.

6. Pound cost averaging

Something many of you will probably not have heard of. In the States of course it's *dollar cost averaging*. And what that means is when you're buying into investments, let's say you're going to buy £5,000 worth of unit trusts, instead of taking a lump of cash and investing it straight off, what you can do is to invest monthly. So let's say you're putting in £100 per month, over 12 months that's £1,200. Well, instead of putting that £1,200 straight in from day one, simply start investing £100 a month at a time. And what that means is, as the price of that financial product goes down you will be, for your £100, actually buying more stock on a monthly basis than if you had put it all in one day one.

If the price goes up, it will work against you in a sense but it's going to be averaged out. As most people don't know whether prices of stocks, bonds, or other investments are going to go up or down, doing it on a monthly basis you are averaging out the cost. If you speak to an Independent Financial Advisor they'll know exactly what this is, anybody in investment markets does, but it is a well-known concept that many of the public don't know about.

7. Compounding

The last of *The 7 Pillars of Wealth Wisdom,* Einstein, the scientist said this is one of the wonders of the world – the most powerful force in the universe. Because if you're a working person starting in their twenties, if you're investing the cost of a £2-something cappuccino a day, a working day, say about £50 a month, it is reckoned over your working life, let's say 30-odd years, by the end of that time you will have a fund worth £1 million.

And it's all because you're getting interest on the interest. Every time the fund increases with interest, the next day the interest will accumulate and a sum will accrue on that interest. It has an exponential effect. Not linear.

So, there we are – 7 Pillars of Wealth Wisdom. Do get to know them, understand them, personally I always refer to them when making a business decision:-

- ✓ *Multiple streams of income*
- ✓ *Income and expenditure flow*
- ✓ *Debt and interest rates*
- ✓ *Tax and government benefits*
- ✓ *Systemising of your business*
- ✓ *Pound or dollar cost averaging*
- ✓ *Compounding*

CHAPTER 3

About the Author

I grew up in relative financial scarcity but experienced the love and caring from my parents growing up in Fulham, West London, which at that time was not terribly prosperous. It certainly wasn't the worst but it was next to Chelsea and Kensington and I went to school in Chelsea. I remember I had a Saturday job like many kids do, in a greengrocers in Chelsea, and I understood that the guys I worked with were working class and yet we were serving in the neighbourhood middle and upper-class families, and I would make deliveries to these families. They were fine but I was acutely aware of the class difference and the wealth difference.

My mother would give me money and I would buy her fruit and veg, oranges and apples, and bring them home and my parents would give me pocket money and a certain amount of money, for my school meals.

I think school meals were subsidised but not free then and I guess on the Sunday night in the front room on the mantelpiece Mum would put our little piles of money, and have a pile for every day, so that was very, very organised and very sensible.

So there was never a lot of money in my house. My father worked for a notary public firm in the City of London, and he came from a very poor working-class family in Hackney, East London, long before gentrification.

There were obviously some genes in the family of intelligence and development. My dad had one brother and two sisters, and the two sisters kind of stayed in the working-class track and eventually they moved from the East End to North London, Edgware.

My father and his brother Tom, they wanted to pull themselves up by their own bootstraps. My Uncle Tom moved to Australia set up a printing business and ended up as the part-time opera correspondent for the *Sydney Evening Herald.*

My father worked his way up in the notary public office to be the manager of the office, but he could never be a partner in the practice because he left school at 14, didn't go to a public school and didn't go to university, and the partners probably went to Oxbridge.

So he didn't come from that social background, and so he could only be managing the business as what they call the Managing Clerk. He could read and speak parts of several languages because the business required knowledge of languages with commercial transactions in the city, foreign imports and exports. My father had a keen sense of humour; he spoke well – he didn't speak with a Cockney accent and there in the office he met my mother who came from rather upmarket Spanish family.

My mother's family came over in the earlier part of the 20th century, and my Spanish grandfather was a diplomat and linguist; he spoke several languages and he had worked in various places in Spain.

My mother, Josefina Pepita, was born in Vigo in Galicia, however the family was from Valencia on the coast in Spain and Grandfather came to the UK. After working in the Spanish embassy in London, he was posted to the Spanish consulate in Scotland. All this was before the Spanish Civil War and a of course we're talking in the 1930s where the Second World War was about to erupt and the Spanish Civil War had taken place between 1936 and 1939, so as the Spanish Civil War finished the second one was started and Europe was not looking too healthy to return to, so the family stayed in the UK.

My Spanish grandfather, Don José Legido O Felan, married a French lady, Ambrosia L'arquier, in Spain, and they spoke Spanish. My grandfather spoke

Castilian Spanish and Valenciano, which is a form of Catalan.

I never knew my grandfather, he died before I was born, but I must say this guy has had a tremendous effect on me, going back to Spain, marrying a Spanish lady, speaking fluent Spanish and digging out our Legido Spanish relatives and cousins who I now know and have regular contact with. Unfortunately none of them are billionaires but hey ho!

So, back to my youth. I went to the London Oratory Catholic School. I failed the 11+ at that time and my mother wanted to get me into a good grammar school, which was actually run by Catholic nuns at the time and halfway through my time there, the nuns were relocated and replaced by civilian teachers, all of whom were very proficient with the cane!

I think I was a smart kid; I got quite a bunch of O-levels or GCSEs but I lacked direction and I must say at that stage I didn't get a lot of support from my parents – they simply wanted the best for me but I think my father was of the view that since he left school at 14, if Martin stays on longer that's all for the good!

So I left school and went into what was called commercial apprenticeship with a woollen importer and manufacturer in Soho in London, run by a Jewish firm called Dick and Goldschmidt, and there I did training and they were very good. I did what was an ONC, an Ordinary National Certificate in business studies, and I spent two years going around departments, in the warehouse, the export department, in the accounts department, and it was a very sensible scheme. You got day release, and I did my ONC and also some A-levels there.

However, at the end of it I thought, *Wooo! Is this all there is?* and I could see that if you didn't have qualifications you were going to be shafted in life!

So I went back to college which was eventually university and I studied law for a while because I had the ONC and A-levels. Eventually I shifted to studying accountancy and I spent some happy few years as a long-haired student joining the Workers' Revolutionary Party and studying capitalist accountancy!

Eventually I got my own qualification in Chartered Accountancy in the five years and I went to work in industry as a financial controller. Didn't know what the hell I was doing, but bit by bit found out what had to be done.

Initially I worked in manufacturing, as a financial controller in the film industry and then for the Civil Aviation Authority, all the time learning and learning.

Finally, I made a conscious decision to move into computing and technology which was clearly the shape of the future arm, and I was offered a job by IBM and Unisys computers. Unisys was one of the bigger companies competing with IBM and I decided to go there on the specific basis that I would be posted to work in one of their overseas subsidiaries.

That led to several happy years, initially based in Amsterdam, Holland, then Rome, Italy, and then working all the time with the head office in New York and Philadelphia, and finally with a spell in the Far East.

I worked in the finance department. I was very much involved in financial planning and also in the marketing department. I was on the high-potential development programme, so again I had some time rotating and working in different departments including human resources, where I was asked to set up a financial training programme, training finance for non-financial people, e.g. sales directors, salesmen, human resources, the IT community and hardware maintenance.

Again, I spent a very happy time whizzing around Western Europe and the States, giving training courses, and this was something that I really, really enjoyed… i.e. the interface with lots of people, their emotions, and helping them along.

Whilst in Amsterdam my wife Teresa and I had our first son, Jan Godfrey, named firstly for his Polish grandfather and secondly because in Holland, Jan (John) is a very common name.

However, all the while I had this entrepreneurial push inside me, moving forward, and at that time I set up with some colleagues in the UK and in Amsterdam a very profitable business. This was of course part-time with my job with Unisys, a business in technology.

This business was at the time of the booming personal computer (PC) market and we initially started to import floppy disks and other peripherals from Hong Kong, and that led to whole PCs, with dot matrix printers. It was a very profitable business which

I sold when I moved out of Holland. It was all based around our favourable import duties into the EEC.

Later I set out a master franchise for an American multilevel marketing business and I successfully set up distributors and again, later sold that business.

After leaving the corporate world and having worked for two other major multinationals in technology and manufacturing, I started my first business in the drinks industry which morphed through various phases from a specialist distributor of mineral water, The Water Club, through to wholesaling a whole range of beers, spirits and soft drinks through to the creation of our own spirit brand, Godfrey's Schnapps, which again in due course was sold for an attractive seven-figure sum!

Unfortunately throughout some of this period Teresa and I were divorced, but have managed to maintain very close contact and support with, by then, my two kids, Jan and Kristiana. Also I had been able to realise my lifelong ambition and actually move over to Spain and live in Barcelona, although many years previously we had been able to buy our first property near to Javea in Spain.

I subsequently made contact with our long-lost LEGIDO relatives and married ANA MUNOZ in Barcelona. Also I was able to realise my ambitions of living by the Mediterranean diving with the PADI course, skiing in winter up in Andorra and the Spanish Pyrenees, really improving my Spanish language, enjoying the cuisine and generally enjoying life! A little bit later, having been a keen sailor and having become a yacht master, I bought my first yacht

– a beautiful classic ketch which after sailing across the Atlantic a few years ago is now based in Grenada in the Caribbean to chase away those winter blues and get some get some heat in the winter!

CHAPTER 4

What Is Wealth to You?

So, what is it that we are trying to create here? What is your definition of wealth? Everyone has their own idea. For many it will be living in a big house, having a superyacht, extensive holidays, living in the sun, driving a big smart car?

Let's not forget, the old international phrase or saying:

to be Healthy, Wealthy, and Wise…

This phrase has translations in

most languages and cultures.

If you want those things these pages and this book will certainly help you, but this is not my intention. My intention is focused on the vast majority who are earning the UK average wage of take-home £1,750 per month and less, and those who are earning a bit more than that who are looking to relieve themselves of the stress of paying a mortgage, paying the rent, paying the utility bills, looking after the kids and putting food on the table. This is my "Why" for writing this book.

- ✓ Did you know that if you are earning £50,000 per annum or more you are in the top 9% of the population?
- ✓ Did you know that if you earn £70,000 or more you are in the top 4% of the population?
- ✓ Did you know that if you are a multi-millionaire you represent .008% of the UK population?
- ✓ Can you imagine what the above figures translated into developing countries around the world would represent? In India, for example, an income of

50,000 per annum puts you in the top .005% of the population.

- ✓ World poverty thankfully has decreased and impressive targets have been achieved but there are worrying signs; economists are very concerned about the widening gap between rich and poor, and the widening skills gap in developing and developed countries between those who will have the skills, assets and abilities to prosper in the new digital economy, and those who will not.
- ✓ So how is wealth created? Statistics vary; in the United States approximately 50% of wealth is created by high-paid jobs, or careers, e.g. high-paid lawyers, top surgeons and medical folk etc. In the UK and Europe 80% of wealth is created through business and only 20% through careers where as in the States 50% is created through business and 50%, as said, through top-paying careers.
- ✓ Did you know in the USA over one third of citizens don't have a pension plan, and don't have savings? To live a decent retirement a "pot" of $300k minimum is required. In the UK this figure would be a "pot" of minimum £250k… and that would not yield much!
- ✓ So this reflects the historical imbalance in the UK and Europe between pay grades for top executives in large companies compared to the USA. This situation has improved markedly from back in the 1970s and early 80s – you could earn a huge amount more in the USA than in the UK, for example. However, this has now evened out over

the last 30-odd years, but still, top pay grades are awarded in the States.

So, the writing is on the wall.

BUSINESS IS THE THING!

We're going to look at ways of developing and monetising financial security in a business-like way, but first we have some basics to cover!

CHAPTER 5

Personal Development

"Knowing others is intelligence; knowing yourself is true wisdom. Mastering others is strength; mastering yourself is true power."

– Lao Tzu – Tao Te Ching

Before you can begin to achieve financial independence it is essential you are in the right place physically and mentally to begin working towards your goal. This means asking yourself some serious questions and getting in the right shape.

You might be thinking you don't need to, you may already be in a good frame of mind and decent health (or think you are, when maybe you're not really), so I recommend you still stay with me on this and ask yourself the questions I pose here. It doesn't take long and it is all part of the process of getting on the road to financial freedom.

So the questions I want you to consider are –

- ✓ ***What is your mental state?***
- ✓ ***What is your attitude to life?***
- ✓ ***How did you grow up?***
- ✓ ***What were the influences?***

These are very important things I want you to look at because they all have a bearing on your very being *right now*. Whether you are aware of it or not, the way you think, your attitude towards life, the influences during your childhood, the education you received, your home life – these are what make you the person you are now.

And that has governed whether you are already in a good, well-paid job or running your own business – or whether you are down on your luck and in minimum wage, long-hours employment.

The great Malcolm Gladwell who wrote *The Tipping Point* and *Blink,* also wrote *The Outliers* in which he analyses the backgrounds of American multi-millionaires of the last century in depth, and such figures as Bill Gates (one of the world's richest men) and many other highly successful entrepreneurs.

And his thesis really is that these people, whilst they might individually be brilliant, there were also certain circumstances in their life that helped shape their destinies, as it were. For instance Bill Gates had middle-class parents and went to a special school, not of course just any school, it was a good school; it was a fee-paying school, a school that had a particular speciality in IT and data processing. And they had an arrangement, the school, with a local data processing centre in the same town, Vancouver. Young Gates was a bit nerdish so the students had the right and ability to spend time in the data processing centre, to go in at the weekends, when the data processing centre wasn't in full flood, or in the evenings, and use the systems and write programs.

Now had Gates gone to a different school that opportunity wouldn't have been there. So Malcolm Gladwell's thesis is that people like Gates, and all these other ground-breaking individuals, they were all subject to these unique and differing factors and circumstances in their lives that helped them in future years to become the innovators they are.

A case in point closer to home, of the 54 total Prime Ministers in the UK, 32 (60%) went to three of the top fee-paying public schools, thus surely demonstrating how background influences future achievements. I have no problem with public schools, in fact my own kids went to them, but I wish their excellent education would be available more widely.

We are all a product, in a way, of our upbringing, environments we grew up in and family backgrounds. We are all subject to these differing conditions and our own specific set of influences.

Now having wonderful opportunities and facilities, well that's all great for Bill Gates, but many of us unfortunately have unpleasant and difficult influences. Maybe there's abuse in the home, maybe there were divorced parents, maybe there were economic problems and many, many people end up, leaving aside social problems, many people have economic ones. I myself grew up in a very scarce but quite loving home, a pleasant home, there was a lot of culture, classical music, literature. My parents talked about cultural things, they were keen tennis players. But there was never ever much money.

My father worked for a firm of notaries in the City of London, this is before the "loadsamoney" lawyer and solicitor culture came in. He came from a dirt poor, really dirt poor family in the East End, in Hackney, again before Hackney became gentrified. There weren't the opportunities there are today. He left school at 14; he was an intelligent chap and he pulled himself up by his own bootstraps, as they say, and got what was considered then a nicer, safer job in an office rather than being out digging up the roads or engaged in heavy manual work, which it was back then as there weren't the power tools around and it was very physically hard work.

So my father did well, he ended up as the manager of the office and speaking languages in a very responsible job. But he was never paid much. They did give him a loan to buy a house which turned out ultimately to be very valuable but he was always bitter about that. He never had much money; he didn't receive much by way of salary increases or bonuses.

As for handling his money, well, he came more from the working-class culture in which people don't pass money down, don't pass wealth on from one generation to the other. He never really saw much need for that; nobody ever gave him any money – why should he give any to us? So from an early age I could see that looking after your money was important.

My mother was a bit different, she came from a Spanish background, she didn't think like that, thank goodness. But generally, it was a very, very frugal childhood that I had and sometimes there wasn't a great deal of food on the table, although there was never rank poverty (I think I would get in trouble with my sister if I were to say there was!)

So, yes – early influences. They play a part in who we become in adult life and looking back I realised that I learned a lot from my father. He looked after his money, what money there was, and had to work hard for what he made. I didn't want to be like that entirely. I knew quite early on that I didn't want to work hard for relatively nothing.

Yes, I did have jobs and I trained as an accountant – but I knew I would not be working for other people all my life. I am not knocking work, it's a good grounding, I just felt there was more I could do to accrue wealth without expending as much time and energy working for others and this is something I explore in greater detail further on in the book.

But enough about me – let us return to you and I want you to consider:

- *What were your influences?*
- *Think about it as you read this page, as you read this book.*
- *Was your home life abundant? Or was there scarcity?*

If you are David Cameron and his colleagues and went to Eton (I believe Eton is charging something over £40,000 a year at the moment) you clearly didn't have a scarce background, did you?

If you grow up in that kind of environment you grow up expecting the best, you're not used to limiting yourself, you expect there to be abundance around you. And of course, with the "elite" and the establishment, there is always abundance. It is very rare that anyone in the higher echelons of society ever falls very far and suffers poverty or hardship. They will never end up on the streets sleeping rough in winter. You get the odd exception now and again but generally speaking wealthy families and individuals usually manage to enjoy their wealth year after year all their life and even down through the generations.

For the rest of us though, much of it is a state of mind. Do we just accept what we have or do we look to do better? There are those who have the drive and determination to make more for themselves – and there are those who are happy just plodding along, getting by. Some may not have too much choice, but many of us do.

AND OF COURSE, WHAT YOU CONTINUALLY DWELL ON, THINK ABOUT,

IS WHAT WILL COME TO PASS!

If you dwell on sleeping on the streets in a sleeping bag and drinking methylated spirits, if you keep dwelling on that, give it a bit of time and you will probably be doing it. And this is fact, it has been proven by great thinkers such as Napoleon Hill who wrote about the power of "auto-suggestion", a method by which you say something often enough, it will come true.

In other words, if you dwell on whatever you are going to dream on, think on, "dwell" I think is a good way of describing it, that will typically come to pass. These are long established facts. Now you may say, "Well, you know, I dream about becoming rich all the time," well okay, maybe you do, but have you really focused on it? Have you really made an effort to make that desire reality?

And that is another important factor – you need a plan to put into action to achieve the wealth you aspire to. It won't just happen (unless you get very lucky on the lottery). So this is another crucial element to ***The Great Book of Wealth Secrets*** and which again is part of the reason for writing this book, as I had a plan and I put it into action and it worked for me.

It can work for you too.

So what I want you to do after reading this book or while you are doing so, is to think about your early influences. I want you to go back in time to explore your personal background, to reflect on what makes you the person you are.

And what I would recommend is that with these recollections you should take some proper time out to reflect. In the next couple of months try and take a day away and if you can go with your partner, your friend, that's all fine but you need some time to yourself, you need some time alone to reflect. Go to the coast, go on holiday to the Mediterranean or wherever or just hang around in your back garden, it doesn't matter, take some time for yourself, think back and try and analyse, try a bit of self-analysis.

Try and analyse what those earlier influences are because believe you me, a lot of those influences are what has made you the person you are now. And if you look at the statistics, they say that even now, even in the womb, the baby is hearing. The baby can hear, the baby is absorbing and learning, even in the womb.

Of course, from the age of zero a baby is sucking stuff up all the time.

So think back, take some time, analyse yourself, think about your earliest memories and upbringing. It may be painful, but that's okay. Work through it, use it. Embrace the experiences you had and realise that they are in the past. If they were bad memories, well, that's okay. You're still here, still alive, all that was in the past. Traumatic maybe, but the chances are the people who were in your life or the environment you were in has changed now. So you can rise above them and stand tall and realise that you are still here and have places to go.

This may well trigger other emotions and feelings. Well, that's okay too. It is good to face these things. And of course you have to start to work to remove some of those negative influences if they are there, and I bet you some of them are.

And take your time too. It's not a race. Allow yourself the space and time to reflect. This is important too. There may be a whole rush of things that will be upsetting or uncomfortable and you have to allow yourself some breathing room to assimilate these feelings and emotions so that you can acknowledge them and understand where they are coming from and make sense of them.

Then you will be able to say, "Ah yes, I see why I am like this…" There will be all sorts of associations coming from these reflection exercises. Many dots to join up possibly.

Or not, as the case may be. Not all of us will have had upsetting pasts and that's good of course, yet you may be surprised how little you know of yourself until you start looking deep inside. You don't necessarily need to have had a bad childhood or family home life to then find yourself as someone who has negative thoughts or behaviour in adult life. Your childhood may have been the happiest ever, yet that doesn't mean to say there won't have been influences that have made you be a cautious person now or one who is always filled with self-doubt or low esteem. There are many factors that may be at root.

Influences are sometimes subtle, that is worth remembering as you begin your reflections.

YOUR EARLY INFLUENCES

So, what do you remember? Have a little think about your family. Did you get pocket money as a kid? What school did you go to? Was it a state school? Private school? If it was state, was it a grammar school, secondary modern? Whatever kind of school, was it good? What were the influences there? Who were the friends you had there? Was there any specialisms in sport, or influences in religion? I went to a Catholic school and there were nuns for quite some time running the school before it changed, so there was a Catholic ambience about the place which I remember quite well and that had an effect on me.

Did you go on to university? Did you have a higher education? If so, maybe you were of my generation, who were actually *paid* to go, as it were, as we received grants to go to uni. Now of course you need to pay for it all. And of course foreign students have to pay a great deal to come here to the UK, but those uni/college days are telling; we experience new things, new people, new ideas and concepts and engage in social interaction that is all different from our school days or family life. So what were these days like for you? Were they enjoyable? Difficult? Have a think and reflect on how they affected you.

What about your first job? Moving on from your family? Think about that.

A former student of mine, for example, his parents divorced. His father was quite abusive, verbally abusive, but on one occasion apparently it got physical. The father was a very intelligent, highly motivated, very Yang sort of guy – I talk in terms of Ying and Yang from my Tai Chi background, I think it's a fabulous way to describe how people act – so Yang is very outgoing, forward, demonstrative, leading and so forth, the father was very much like that.

And even though they separated, the father paid for this chap to go to a private school. So off he went every morning with his cap and blazer and nice tie and his satchel, however, his mother and the child were living on a council estate, so he would get abused by the local toughs. And if you sit and talk to this chap you can see very closely those influences. He's tense, he's nervous, he can't really drink coffee because he would start flying off through the roof; highly intelligent but very much affected.

Maybe you had a similar experience? The point is, it's good to know yourself (if you don't already). But even if you do think you know yourself, go through this exercise anyway as it really is the starting position for going on to make the most of this book and all things we will be looking at.

The Great Book of Wealth Secrets depends on making a fresh start, it's like beginning your life again in a way, wiping the slate clean, revaluating, analysing, finding new focus, adopting new attitudes, embracing new practices, utilising fresh ideas and methods.

It is all important and part of my *wholistic* approach.

Okay, so keeping the theme going, let's move on to your job.

JOBS

What are your earliest recollections? What sort of job did you have? Did you have a Saturday job? A newspaper round? One of my first jobs was working for a greengrocer's in Kensington and Chelsea. And it was good, but it also reinforced a little bit the scarcity in our house because I was delivering groceries to some very, very wealthy households in Kensington and Chelsea. Our house wasn't that different but it wasn't half as abundant as some of the ones I saw and delivered to, and that was striking to me. I got a feel of what else there was out there in terms of what wealth was and what you could achieve financially. It was a good time ago so people were more stratified than they are now, the class system was far more evident here in the UK than it is today.

So ask yourself, how were you made to feel about money and wealth in your home and in your job?

At the end of this chapter you will be asked to write down ten of the influences you had – five positive and five negative – when you were growing up. This will get you thinking and start opening your mind again. It's all part of the process of your personal regeneration that I want to help take you through.

If that sounds deep – well, it has to be in all honesty, as it is the only way to shake off the cobwebs and start life again, refreshed and with new vigour and purpose. It is the only way if you want to achieve financial freedom.

And remember, that is the whole purpose of this book.

MAKING CHANGES

So, how do we go about making changes? How do we do that? Well, I think it's all about re-educating ourselves to a large degree. We all go through the school process, the education system, and that, let's be honest, is pretty much dictated by the state, the government. The curriculum is decided by people who think they know what's best for us and we are more or less forced to learn these things that they want us to learn. We don't have a choice.

We move on to further education, college, university and suddenly our eyes are opened a little more as we get to start using our minds more and begin to question and explore for ourselves. And that's good, of course.

But even into adulthood and we are very much still a part of the "system" that is in place, run by the state, the government who still make policies and laws and decide what they think is best for us, whether we agree or not. We are still told what to do, how to behave, what is allowed and what isn't. That's all fine, of course, a society needs structure to be able to function.

The point is, we are not totally free unless we start to think for ourselves and it is only by thinking for ourselves that we can really achieve financial independence. So making changes depends a lot on educating ourselves, finding out about things for ourselves.

And that can we can do now, even more than ever. As they say, you're never too old to learn and we never stop learning. It's true. There is always something new to discover, about yourself or about the wider world in general.

So how do we do this?

Reading books? Reading articles on the Internet? Watching YouTube or videos? In a word – yes.

The thing is, there's so much and if anything there is probably too much information out there. I sometimes feel we're going through information overload and you probably do too. I actually find it quite astounding, the massive amounts of digital information there is today but I have to say it's something I really love. Wikipedia isn't that great. An online encyclopaedia? They say it's not always 100% accurate, but goodness me considering the pages are basically created by individuals like you and I, as well as academics, I find it incredibly useful and it at least provides a starting point if you were looking for information on someone or something. It's a quick resource and reference guide that I find invaluable.

For instance, you could be watching a television program or hearing something on the radio or watching something on the Internet and you might think, *Ah, I'd like to check out that person or check out that country or check out that fact*, and with Wikipedia, which is free for goodness' sake, you can do exactly that. You can find out about almost anything. You can very quickly on your phone just check it out. It's just astounding the amount of data that is available to us now that wasn't there 30 years ago. I mean it is wonderful, a great innovation and public resource.

I like to donate to it because it's such a wonderful resource that didn't exist before. I use it a lot and so I like to support it as it is free from adverts, so relies on donations to keep the site going and information updated and maintained. Free from adverts – now what's not to like?

And so, books are there. I like to read paper versions, and you've got online versions too like Kindle and so on. YouTube, again, is the second largest search engine after Google web searching where you can find video clips on just about anything out there right now. And it's very, very informative, the Internet generally.

My point is, you may be someone who only uses the Internet for social media or emailing or watching movies or listening to music or comparing prices of products and services or booking an air flight. That's all fine, of course, what I am saying is you should start getting used to utilising the Internet in other ways.

For research in other words and information gathering – for education purposes. And this will make more sense later on in the book, because using the Internet will feature quite heavily in due course.

MENTORING

Now, although I have just talked about self-educating and re-educating, I do appreciate that not everyone will be comfortable with this or have the confidence to trust themselves. And that is understandable. It's not easy to learn for ourselves for we can't always be sure the material we are looking at can be trusted. So some of us may decide we need a guiding hand and that is where mentoring can help.

Mentoring is reckoned to be one of the most effective ways to go forward if you are taking steps on a new path and many people find it very useful because it enables you to really focus. A book you can put down or you can switch off your computer, but if you are working with somebody for a day or a few days or continually, it's a whole different mind-set.

I have a life coach, a guy called George Metcalfe who was one of the first life coaches in the UK. He is tremendously spiritual and we have worked together for almost 20 years and he has helped me get where I am today. Mentoring works, because for the period of time you are being mentored you have to focus and there is something immensely creative that comes from that process, two minds – one plus one, equals 3, 5, 10.

You can find mentors for all kinds of areas of life and needs. From personal development to business. There are Master-Mind Groups and Circle Groups which help people looking for business mentoring or you can go for one-on-one. The point is, mentoring really works and helps to drive you forward.

TRAINING

Training of course is very valuable if you are setting off on a new road, whether it is to update or improve the skills you already possess, or if you have decided to pursue a new career or trade and are starting from scratch.

After all, ignorance can be extremely expensive, so general training programs can be very useful.

The UK government is very keen on training at the moment and is trying to take things further forward. At the end of the following chapter there will be training resources for you to access, but of course there are new training programs and online courses becoming available all the time so it is always good to check what is out there for yourself. Online courses are often a lot cheaper too than physical, on-site training sessions. That of course is because there are far fewer overheads involved for the training provider, those cost-savings being transferred to the student.

YOUR NETWORK IS YOUR NET WORTH

Mixing with the right folk, in other words. Some of you may have heard the phrase before – "Your network is your net worth." I heard it about 15 years ago and thought, *What does that mean? What's that all about?* And now I understand it because, to put it bluntly, if you hang around deadbeats you are likely to be influenced and could end up a deadbeat yourself.

If that sounds a bit heavy, well, I make no apology because it's true. Being around negative people and negative environments does nothing but bring one down. It's inevitable. You cannot *not* be affected by negativity. It's just not possible, unless you are very strong of character and can override anything at all. But even that takes effort, so why put yourself in that position in the first place? Exactly, there is no point.

But if you hang around positive, energetic, intelligent folk who are going somewhere – and that can include folk who have wealth, though that's not an essential thing – you will find it very positive and life affirming.

I for one need to be around interesting people. I can't stand hanging around boring people who, with the greatest respect to football, can only talk about football in the pub and like to down several pints while doing it – that's all right every once in a while, yeah, no problem at all, but if that is the main raison d'être for your life, it's not good. I would even say it's a bit pathetic.

So interesting folk, intelligent folk, folk with energy – these are the people you want to be getting into your network and we'll be going into existing methods and networks out there in the UK for you to do that, and you can see them at the end of the chapter.

Personally, I have been involved in many networks over the past few years as my own business interests expanded. I'm talking about the likes of WIBN.co.uk, the Institute of Directors, www.iod.com; there's big organisations, various building establishments in London, there's a big one off Trafalgar Square, in the Mall, a modernistic one and a more traditional one. It's great to meet other directors and like-minded folk, on a mission, going somewhere. I used to be a member of that, but I am not a member right now, but networking is important and we'll be putting up more resources for you to refer to.

That's at the top business end of course, there are all kinds of networks you can join pertinent to your own employment or trade or skill and it is well worth joining one because, as with the principles behind mentoring, it's good to talk and share experiences and receive advice or encouragement. Again, it's about learning, really, and you can never do enough of that, believe me.

And I think it's good too that there's fantastic business network opportunities like LinkedIn and Facebook which are highly useful and very popular. LinkedIn is an amazing resource for connecting with new people and finding like-minded associates, but trust me, there's something magical about meeting face to face – I'm talking about energetic transference; when you look at somebody, energy. They say that the eyes are the window to the soul; when you look at somebody, you gaze, and you engage with them, there is an energy transfer. You just don't get that with LinkedIn or Facebook, not really.

LIFE FORCE

I mentioned the word "righteous" earlier. That has many variations – virtuous, moral, good, just, upright, honourable, honest, respectable, decent, blameless. I try to live my life that way, following those principles. And I do that because I think it is important and has helped me in my quest to be financially independent.

I find it's all part of the whole that keeps me functioning well and productively day by day. It's all part of feeling good about yourself, because ultimately when you do you can go and achieve anything. When you are fully attuned to yourself, with a clear mind and steady heart, you are in the perfect place to focus on your goals and be better able to accomplish them.

I have been practising and teaching Tai Chi and Qi Gong for many years now. The Chi – or rather "Qi" to use the proper Chinese pronunciation – translates as "breath", "air", or "gas", but also figuratively as "life force" or "energy flow".

So in relation to networking, meeting people, there is an element of Tai Chi in that you can sense pretty much right away, whether the person repels you or it can really lock you in a good relationship from the off.

Physical touch is important too; if you shake hands, the Spanish use the term *abrazo*, a hug. It's not quite the same as a hug though. They use it all the time, if you know somebody and it's a formal relationship you end a letter or an email by saying *suyo fielmente* – yours faithfully. If it's a friendly person, a colleague or family member, you could say *saludos* – salutations. But often they would use *un abrazo* and often they will hug; the Latins do that and actually that makes a difference. Warm, friendly, it's positive, when you see it in action more often or not you will see plenty of smiles too. Again following Malcolm Gladwell's line – everything counts.

Which brings me to Brian Tracey. I did a course created by Brian Tracey some 20 years ago. Brian Tracey is very deeply powerful, he is a leading light in sales training, he does all sorts of training; he's been on the scene a long time and he's written a lot of books. I had an old tape course given to me by a New Zealand friend who did a course of his and the last section of the tape, he goes through the various laws of the universe, the so-called law of attraction which was made such a big thing of a few years ago, the secret.

But at the end of the last tape, he said –

EVERYTHING COUNTS.

And I find it's true.

The person who is sitting next to you right now as you're reading this book. The person you are about to meet when you get off the train, where you're walking through, you might be at Kings Cross St. Pancras station, wherever, everything counts in your life. Maybe right at that moment or maybe it will be the next day or week or month or year or many years in the future. You never know. It might be something you see, something someone says in passing, a piece of information you pick up randomly, an experience that will provide lesson somewhere down the line. It all counts. It's all good stuff. So take note of it all because everything counts, right then and there but not only in the here and now.

Start to think in terms of that, because what we are aiming to do as we're now getting into this, we are aiming to construct the life that you want; to build the life that you want. To manifest the life that you want – attuned, in alignment with the universe because, I'll put my cards right on the table now, I believe there is a higher power – and I'm not talking religion here – I am saying, in my view, from my experiences in life, there is a higher power.

I personally have had a number of experiences which lead me to make this statement. Believe me, it's not a frivolous statement, I can assure you. There is a higher power, a loving higher power which we can lock into and attune to, providing our thoughts and our intentions are honourable, ethical, and righteous. I like that word, "righteous". It's good, isn't it? Providing it's righteous, we can lock in and the universe will help us.

Okay, so we're still looking at how we can develop ourselves and really it is all leading to creating a situation, an environment, where you can achieve an abundant and happy life.

AN ABUNDANT & HAPPY LIFE

I think without question this is what we all want, everyone wants, deep down inside. Isn't it? We would all love to have a happy life and one that is abundant with not only wealth, but well-being too. As I have said many times already, that can be achieved through financial independence. And this is the ultimate aim – an abundant and happy life.

So what are the elements that you need for an abundant and happy life? As I mentioned earlier, you need to have the right attitude, an abundant attitude, a warm and loving attitude. This is my view, but I hope by the way, that nothing you read in this book is new. Some of it will be new to some of you, but I really fervently hope that none of it is because much of it is common sense really, things you know already that have probably been buried or lost within you, hiding under the surface.

Let's start with **Repetition**. *You need repetition.* Repetition is an essential element in life and many of us absolutely, me included, require repetition to drive points home; to stress points so that we fully understand them and become aware of them. That's why when people are giving speeches, the master speech makers, they typically repeat things three times. There's a comfort factor in there with repetition and it's necessary if you want to take control of your life and live an abundant and happy life.

Attitude is another one – *the right attitude to life.* How do you feel about yourself? You must be feeling good about yourself. You need to feel good about your fellow man as well. If you're bitter, rancorous and are harbouring lots of negative hatred towards others, jealousy is another really bad one, it's going to be difficult for you to have a happy and abundant life and at the end of the day that's what people want, I believe, they just want peace. They want peace and I don't mean just a peaceful life sitting under a palm tree, some people want to be climbing mountains or doing extreme sports and things like that, but really it's all about *inner peace*, I believe, that is what we are all looking for, you're looking to be comfortable in our own skins; comfortable with ourselves. And I believe that if you were to think about you would say the same too.

You need to feel who you really are because every one of us is an individual, we were made individually. We have our own thoughts, our own strategies. We are all different… and thank goodness for that. You need to be living in the moment, not worrying, not living in the past. When you were brought up in the 50s, 60s, 70s, 80s, things were a bit different. There are eras, things do change. You only have to look at the Internet and how that has changed things so much.

However, the *essence of life* I believe stays the same, it's the influences around us that are changing and have changed. So, don't worry about the past, the past's gone. Tomorrow? You don't know what's going to happen tomorrow. Live in the moment, now. Relish it. Cherish it. Enjoy it. Absolutely enjoy the moment so that you can get the maximum from the here and the now.

THIS IS THE WAY YOU NEED TO LIVE

Think of your self-image. You need to think around that. How do you project yourself? Do you project yourself as a friendly bunny, an aggressive person? What impact do you have on other people? How do others react to you?

There's also your physical image. What do you look like? Do you look after yourself? I always look at people's shoes, I can't help it. Somebody might be looking very smart but they're wearing a pair of cheap shoes it kind of spoils the image. I have always paid attention to it, not that I am dilettante, it's just that I'm aware of the image we create. And of course body language, the way we stand, the way we react to people, the way we move, the way we walk. Are we slumped? Are we upright? Do we project a positive image?

Above all and the main point about this is how you feel about yourself.
How do YOU feel about yourself?
Ask yourself, seriously.

Okay, next thing – **Giving Thanks**. It's a very polite thing to do, isn't it? But it's also a very spiritual thing to do. If you give thanks to others around you, friends, family, people you meet in the street, people you meet in shops – thank them. The checkout person in a supermarket, thank them for the work they are doing there, they are probably not being paid very much and they appreciate the thanks.

I was at an airport recently, Gatwick, and there was a young police woman there with a huge machine gun and I went up to her and said, "Thank you for protecting us." And she was chuffed. I have a colleague who is in the diplomatic protection squad and is fully arms-trained and so forth, and he said to me, "We really appreciate it when members of the pubic actually thank us because, you know, it can be a thankless job."

So thank people for what they are doing because giving thanks helps you to focus on the positive, doesn't it? You know, just coming back to the analogies of the supermarket, you may be in a checkout line, you could get bitter and could be thinking, *Damn, I wish he (or she) would speed up so I can get checked out and get on my way quicker,* and you could be bitter and rancorous about that, couldn't you? But on the other hand, you could thank them for doing a good job; perhaps the queue was moving slowly because the checkout person was taking the time to help out an older member of the community. There are often reasons, small reasons, why things are being delayed and you are being held up. So being aware of what is around you and accepting that it is okay, there is no need to get uptight about it, appreciating what others might be doing for others helps you to stay positive and calm. Be thankful that others care.

Pay attention to your **Body**. The body contains the soul, your mind, look after it. What are you doing – are you abusing it with drugs, with too much alcohol? Do you smoke? Stop that if you are, who amongst you is still smoking? That has got to be the biggest mug's game out there. Alcohol – there's huge amounts of proof now from the medical community that alcohol is cancer-inducing, particularly in some instances with women and breast cancer. If you speak with a doctor or nurse you'll find out, even that wonderful glass of wine, well, maybe one glass is okay. But alcohol is generally considered to be harmful right now, and unfortunately too many people drink too much. I used to drink socially but found that I was drinking too much so cut right back and have virtually stopped.

So think about the body.

Take **Exercise**. You don't need to go to a gym, you can do exercise at home, you can go walking, there's all these apps to help you now to count the number of steps you are doing. A few thousand a day you are meant to be doing. Look after your body because it is the receptacle of your spirit and mind.

Forgive. Forgive people. Don't hold on to grudges. If you hold on to grudges, it's negative thoughts. They will eat away at you and you will become bitter and twisted. So forget it, forgive. Nobody's perfect – some people come close perhaps – but most people do make errors and often there's no intention to do anything to harm you but errors are made and my strong advice to you is, it's not just mine, these views have come through the ages, coming out of the Bible, the Quran, the I Ching – forgive. And the flipside of forgiving is actually *giving*.

Give To Others. It's wonderful. As human beings we are programmed, contrary to popular belief, I believe we are programmed to enjoy and feel fulfilled when we help others and giving, and I am not just talking about money – although there's nothing wrong with giving money, donating, huge amounts are donated every year to charities – give your time, you will feel good for it. And I think most people reading this will probably understand that.

So give. Have **Goals**. Goals have a power. Again, there have been books and tomes written on this. The famous study at Stanford in the 1970s for instance – they got one bunch of students to sit down and write out their goals for the next 20 years, broken down into years, months, and weeks, and the other group didn't – and they got the two groups together after 20 years and the people who had written down their goals, would you believe, and you probably know I am going to say this, but they had actually achieved a lot more in their lives than the ones who didn't write their goals down.

Goals have a power, writing them down, they have a power, the written word. It can be a typed word, a spoken word. *Everything counts.* And putting them down on paper, putting them down in a digital file, it is important. It helps you to dwell on those goals.

And I, well I'm not brilliant at it, sometimes I set goals for myself, sometimes I don't. When I do and I don't achieve them they are actually quite painful to look at. But on the whole, having goals and setting out to achieve them, and reaching them, it works, it is fulfilling, it gives you a sense of achievement. It is satisfying and rewarding, you get a very positive feel-good buzz. It is a very positive practice to adopt so I do recommend it wholeheartedly. It's just that sometimes we forget to do it. Remind yourself to do it – as I said earlier – repetition is good. Make goal-setting a habit and it will soon become second nature.

That may all sound very serious so far, so also remember that **Humour** is important. We all need to enjoy a smile regularly. So *have a sense of humour.* There's nothing too serious in life. Humour is a very magical thing. Having a good sense of humour is great, it enlightens other people, it enlightens their day. It makes you popular as opposed to somebody who is grumpy and being around people who make you smile and laugh, it's fun, makes you feel good. And I firmly believe the universe made us to have fun and to enjoy life; having a good sense of humour is part of the magical aspect of being a human being that we have. I am not too sure whether other animals have that. But we do.

RELATIONSHIPS

The kind of relationships you have, good relationships, being with the right people, fostering relationships with your family, it's a very important aspect of maintaining your sense of well-being. I mentioned earlier that your work or business networks are your net worth, they are necessary if you are to be successful in life from a financial and career point of view but your personal-life relationships are equally as important. Ideally, you will have a happy balance of both to help maximise your overall abundance for a happy life.

I believe, again, the universe smiles on people with harmonious relationships and that burrows through, in my view, into wealth because you see there's no cast-iron, concrete rules about anything but you do notice that folk who do have stable home lives – Richard Branson for example, I believe has been married to the same lady for many, many, many years – are predominantly happy and enjoying an abundant life.

He has support, he has backup. Theo Paphitis from Dragon's Den, again married quite young, stable home life, support from a loving partner. So relationships, very, very important. And if you think relationships, like I used to, have nothing to do with business, then I believe you're wrong. They are all part of the same thing, intertwined.

EVERYTHING COUNTS

Finally, have **Faith**. I do believe one needs to have faith in the higher power. I don't believe this universe just rocks and rolls by itself. I believe there is a force out there. It's entirely up to you, I'm not trying to ram this down anybody's throat and I am not talking specific religions, but I do believe there is a power that we can tune into.

Let's stop for a moment and think what's out there. We've got probes going up there now, photos of Pluto, Mars, but that's just one amongst billions of planets and what's beyond the billions of planets? The Big Bang Theory? What more? Where and how was all this created? I get a bit cross-eyed when I try and think about it as I find the universe to be an absolutely incredible, amazing thing, it is mind boggling and we really only know a mere fraction of what it is all about, the depths involved. Infinity? If there is such a thing, well, it's just a mind-blowing concept, I find. And if you think in those terms then, in reality, anything is possible.

We make it so hard for ourselves generally, many of us. Life is a wonderful thing, but we can make it so complicated. Maybe we overthink things too much? But then they do say that the simplest things are the hardest to do.

And that may be why we tend to forget all the simple things that can give us an abundant and happy life.

RECAP

✓	***Repetition***	✓	***Forgive***
✓	***Attitude***	✓	***Give***
✓	***Self-Image***	✓	***Goals***
✓	***The Body***	✓	***Relationships***
✓	***Giving Thanks***	✓	***Faith***

As you may know, there is a website we are launching with this book which we call *The Wealth Tree* (or TWT for short). It's an offshoot of the thoughts and ideas I am expressing here and has been designed as a resource and practical guide for everyday use offering up-to-date information on the things I am covering in this book.

We have looked at Personal Development, in the following chapters we turn our attention to protecting your wealth and then how to go about creating more wealth.

RESOURCES

Some Classics

- *Awaken The Giant Within, How To Take Immediate Control Of Your Mental, Emotional, Physical and Financial Life* : Anthony Robbins
- *Think and Grow Rich*: Napoleon Hill
- *The 4 Hour Working Week, Live Anywhere and Join The New Rich*: Tim Ferris
- *Rich Dad, Poor Dad*: Robert Kyosaki
- *How To Stop Worrying and Start Living*: Dale Carnegie
- *The 7 Habits Of Highly Effective People*: Stephen Covey

And More:

- *Feel The Fear And Do It Anyway*: Susan Jeffers

- *The Universe Has Your Back*: Gabrielle Bernstein
- *You Are a Bad Ass*: Jen Sincero

CHAPTER 6

How To Keep What You've Got

"What we call our destiny is truly our character and that character can be altered. The knowledge that we are responsible for our actions and attitudes does not need to be discouraging, because it also means that we are free to change this destiny."

– *Anaïs Nin*

So, focusing on the roots of The Wealth Tree, what have we got? We've got, firstly, a very obvious but nevertheless essential component – *spending.* If that made you groan, then that is very telling. That hit a nerve, did it? Good.

PLANNING YOUR SPENDING

This is about looking after what you've got. Planning your spending, controlling what you spend. Makes sense, doesn't it? But how often do we take note of this simple practice? Hardly ever? That would be about right, for most of us. But it is easy to see why we fall into that spending trap as there is something offered to us all too easily that we grab with both hands eagerly. Can you guess what it is? I expect you can. Yes, that's right – CREDIT (and we'll be looking at credit in greater depth in a moment).

For now, let us go back to basics. Controlling your spending. It's important for many reasons and it can be achieved easily, with a bit of practice. The words I like to use are – be frugal. Not cheap. Be frugal. Don't *waste* money. Spend your money on the things you really want to spend it on (after thinking about it, and thinking about it carefully). And that can mean if you really want something really badly like a holiday, to go down the Nile or if you're a fashionista female and want to buy some really cool clothes and they're expensive and designer, a Versace dress or something, well right, get your money aside saved for that and spend it on those things.

To do that, you are best off setting a plan, a proper plan. One you can follow, repeatedly. Daily, weekly, monthly. It's not for everybody; some people like to do this, a lot of people do it. You can set one up yourself on Excel. If not, we will be giving out resources again at the end of this chapter. There are online resources; you can download free software to set up planning. One of them is a piece of software called Mint.

And in this area Microsoft Money has done research, in fact there has been a lot of research in this area and they call this the MSN Money 60% and they break it down like this:-

- Investments, pensions, ISA, savings – **20%** of your income
- Saving up for holidays, deposit for a house, gifts – **10%**
- Your fixed costs, rent, mortgage, utilities, credit card, daily spending and living expenses – **60%**
- And then fun spending, clothes, entertainment, fun, restaurants, theatre etc. – **10%**

So obviously that's going to vary between individuals, you may want to do things slightly differently, but basically the key elements are that you are going to have a certain amount for general living expenses, a certain amount for savings and investments, and then the money you put aside for holidays and fun times, and that should be around 5-10%, but I would say try and make the frivolous part of it, if you're just starting out and are in real trouble, with real difficulties, try and keep that down to 5%.

Basic stuff, very basic stuff. And apologies if you feel this is too basic, but we often, and I certainly do, need reminding of these things just to keep focus on them. I mentioned earlier a system called Mint, another one is You Need A Budget (YNAB). GNU Cash. Money Dance. These you can find online.

So that's controlling your spending by planning what you will be spending on and what percentage of your income you allocate to certain elements of your life.

CREDIT CARDS

This is a much abused area for the simple fact that it is all too easy to get credit these days and all too enticing to apply for it. I should know, I do it and have done it a lot over the years. I don't blame anyone for using credit as it is incredibly useful and helpful for many millions of people for a variety of reasons throughout history and the time when usury was first introduced to mankind.

Now you may think: *What? Surely credit is a bad thing to rely on and use, it only adds to my financial obligations.* This of course is very true and it is a question of balance really. The thing is, moneylenders WANT YOU TO HAVE CREDIT so they make it attractive in the first place, but at the same time they want you to MANAGE YOUR BORROWING and keep it under control and these days your credit is monitored far more effectively. The last thing they want is people going bankrupt, so they will always try to ensure you don't borrow more than you can afford to pay back.

A few years ago, a decade or so, that was not the case, the credit industry was very lax and it was easy to get credit cards at the drop of a hat. I personally know someone who had an astonishing 18 different credit cards. He had a respectable job and then retired but somehow he had racked up huge debts with all these cards to the tune of £73,000. He had no choice but to go bankrupt. He had recently got married again which added to his shame, and his new wife was in total shock as she knew nothing about the debts which he had accrued *before* marrying her. His whole life changed. He no longer had any means of withdrawing any money and had to rely on his wife to manage his pension income and give him cash, of which he was allowed very little. Originally, his bankruptcy was to last three years, but after just twelve months that "sentence" was reduced to just one year. Whether he was allowed to get credit again I don't know, but I know it was a salutary lesson he learned. If ever there was an example of not being financially free, this is it. It's the complete opposite, in fact, of financial independence.

So the absolute moral of this story is CREDIT is useful, it is not a crime to use it but you must treat it with respect and not get sucked into debt. There are some very easy ways to do this:-

CHECK YOUR CREDIT CARD AND CHECK YOUR CREDIT RATING.

It's a good idea to find out properly, "officially", where you stand with your credit card or cards but also what your actual credit rating is. This is something people don't do very often; they may not really know about it, but everyone is in the "system" so to speak as far as what their credit history is and total debts amount to. Everyone has a credit file.

Items will come up on your credit file so you really need to check yourself out on Experian, EquiFact, Check My File, Noddle – they're all subscription-based or free, and a useful way to gauge your current rating. However, be careful as these things do cost. Experian is something like £15 a month which is ridiculous and I think somewhat abusive, you don't need to go in that often. For a couple of pounds now I think you can phone them or write in and ask them to send it to you, you have the right under data protection to be given your credit rating for only two pounds, so why pay £15 a month when you really don't need to? Wherever you go people will make money from money. There are now various free programs to get your credit data.

YOUR CREDIT FILE

So your credit file will contain things like how long you have lived in your current dwelling. Are you on the electoral role? (You should be for that is the start of all the credit checking.) Are you on the Royal Mail post code address file? How long have you actually lived where you are currently registered? Have you had any court actions, do you have CCJ (County Court Judgments) against you? Have you been bankrupt? What is your credit history generally? Who do you owe money to? How much do you owe to those lenders, for example your mortgages, your credit cards? Certainly now Lloyds Bank and others are putting information of any borrowings into these credit files. Not all banks do that, so it's a good tip to try and make sure you find a bank that does not give information to those who are keeping the credit file. Why should you offer more information than is really necessary?

You will get warnings of any fraudulent activity on some of the systems, any fraudulent applications that the systems come up with, which is necessary of course as these days there's a lot of concern about identity theft. If you've had credit at a certain address and then moved away, that will come up, but anyone who then becomes connected to that property might become a problem for you indirectly.

I have an address on a buy-to-let property that I own and for some reason just that one property is connected with me. Obviously tenants living there don't have my surname, they don't have my name, so it's not too much of a concern but nonetheless it makes me feel a bit uncomfortable. I have tried to get it changed on more than one occasion but for some reason, and maybe I haven't tried hard enough, it hasn't gone away. If you have connected people in your residence be careful because there might be an overspill if they have any bad credit.

There's a whole range of different levels of checks that are done. They talk about footprints going all over your credit file and the very fact that you have applied for credit, even if you haven't got it, haven't been granted it, can count against you. A bit of a dark art here, different lenders or different companies, Experian and others, do things in different ways, but applying for credit can affect your credit. Even you looking at your own record may under certain circumstances affect your file.

SO HOW IS YOUR CREDIT SCORE ARRIVED AT?

Because you realise there is a credit score, Experian for example has a credit score that goes from 0 to 1000. If you're at 700 that's considered quite good, if you're below 500 that's considered not to be good. Below 300 is bad but you can easily get scores of 999 and so forth.

So they do it in different ways and they don't disclose exactly how it is done, but roughly the score is worked out in the following ways:

30% of your credit score is based on stability.

The number of years you have lived at your current address. Do you own the property or are you renting it? If you're renting it and have lived there for a good chunk of time, that's considered acceptable and it's stability. Obviously if you're young and just starting out on your credit journey it's more difficult to create a good and long-established credit file though age can actually count in your favour in that respect.

Payment history is another 30%.

So if you have credit cards I would recommend you have direct debits set up from your bank account so at least the minimum payment goes in. You may want to have direct debits that pay off the full balance and that's always advisable especially these days with ridiculously low interest rates on lendings. If you are borrowing or investing in products with banks and other financial institutions you're not going to get much money, are you? Maybe a couple of per cent, three per cent if you're lucky. Bank of England base rate is of course 0.75% and it's been low since May 2009, so here we are in the ninth year of that, and every month when the Bank of England Committee meets there's always reporting on whether or not it's going to go up.

It has only increased marginally in nine years, so returns from investments with banks is pitifully low, but conversely, credit cards are still charging anything from 6 per cent, but the average is probably somewhere between 12 to 18 per cent, ridiculous. They will say it's because of the risk associated with credit card lending. So 30% is payment history; if you missed a payment, or paid late, or paid short, and left balances outstanding on your credit report you will see, if everything is green on it with ticks all over the place that is good; if they're orange that's not very good, if they're red that's bad.

So you've got 30% stability, 30% payment history.

20% is based on any court actions and aforementioned CCJs, county court judgments that have been placed against you by any creditors.

Clearly if you have moved around and have a very common name, these systems are all-encompassing so it has been known for some people to disappear from one address. We're in the property rental business and we know lots and lots of tenants who just leave; they don't leave a forwarding address, they don't have their mail forwarded and they just leave everything behind.

So, if they have had a common address and they can't be found elsewhere, their credit file will stay behind at the old address but if they're found it will be linked. So 20% is court actions and that is a very important thing and you want to avoid that at all costs.

10% is credit activity.

How active are you? On the one hand you'll get marked down if you have poor credit, but on the other hand you can also get marked down for not having any credit at all. So again, if you're a student and just starting out and you haven't taken out much credit that's not good either because they can't judge you, they can't see you, you're kind of invisible in the systems.

So they like you to have credit and they like you to have good credit but not no credit. You might think you would be applauded for spending cash and not using credit at all, but actually that is not the case.

10% relates to linked relationships.

Also, your post code. If you live in a difficult area shall we say, and they know that living around you are people who have social problems and are creating debt and are not paying it off, that can count against you as well, so that's a further 10 per cent.

So that's roughly how credit scores are calculated.

Okay, on to credit cards now and something I call the *Credit Card 10 Commandments* as there are, to my mind, ten things you really should be doing to keep your credit card debt under control while at the same time taking advantage of what credit cards can offer. Credit cards can be valuable for all sorts of financing if handled well, which some people do, though as we have seen, some people don't and get caught out.

THE CREDIT CARD 10 COMMANDMENTS:

1. Get all fees waived
2. Negotiate a lower APR
3. Check the market regularly
4. Close credit cards
5. Keep cards a long time
6. Keep them active
7. Use any rewards
8. Beware of cashbacks
9. Get more credit under control
10. Pay off monthly

1. Believe it or not this does work. Phone them and get your fees waived, cancelled. Just about all credit card companies are online now. Personally, I have a few cards. I am only using one at the moment. I like paperless, so I go online and receive all statements online rather than in the post. But there's something about phoning them that seems to work in terms of getting more out of them in your favour. So they will send you offers online and they will also send you offers in paper, if you are still receiving post from them, but even if you are receiving paperless statements they will still send you paper solicitations offering you more credit. That is a given.

They want to lend to you. If you have a decent credit limit or credit rating they want you to borrow. So phone them up, be in contact with them, send them an email, but probably better phoning, and if there are any fees on the card, ask for them to be waived, cancelled. If you don't ask, you don't get. There's a phrase around that says, "The more you play, the more they pay."

2. Phone them up and negotiate a lower APR. You might say to them, "I'm thinking of, or going to close the account, can you give me a better APR?" They won't like that. They want to keep you. Every customer is profit to them ultimately, even if they do play ball and reduce fees or reduce the APR. The fact they have you is what matters to them and they want to keep you. So, basically, play the game and watch them play with you, and they will, believe me.

3. Check the market regularly for the best deals – and check out Martin Lewis the money saving expert, he is fantastic. He started some years back, but has built up a fantastic advice service that is on the people's side. It's good to have a consumer organisation that genuinely tells you how it is and what it all means. I believe he is completely on our side, on the consumer's side and goodness me, isn't there a need for that? There are other sites out there as well, but I really like Martin Lewis, I think he's a bit of a champion actually and good luck to him. So check the market regularly for best deals, you may want to be closing cards and opening others. And if you've got a good credit score that will all be in your favour. I recently asked for a specific credit card for spending abroad and it was the Halifax Clarity Card which Martin had focused on and highlighted as being appropriate for spending on holiday. I am in Europe a lot of the time so that was ideal for me and my Lloyds debit card was putting in additional charges for every transaction that went through in Euros. So that worked well. I only asked for £1,000; I didn't want any credit at all really but I asked for £1,000 and they gave me £9,000! Of course there is a potential downside to that. So beware. Living within your means is extremely important and we will be looking at that in more detail later.

4. Closing credit cards is a good option – but that doesn't mean you can't then open another, especially if there is a good deal going. So, check the deals, close accounts when you don't want them is my view, but again that's controversial. Some people will say keep the cards open and not use them, or use them and pay them off. I think paying them off is the very best strategy, but make sure, as I said before, direct debits are set up; the last thing you want is to miss a payment. So if you're going to do it, do it properly. I believe in closing cards if you're not using them, you may want to keep them open for a while, but do play the system.

5. Keep cards for a long time. I think this whole thing of stability and longevity is important, and if you are using the cards, keep them for some time. It gives you more of a track record.

6. Keep them active as this too looks good on your record, and keeping your repayments up to date of course is another plus.

7. And if there's any rewards offered – though I'm always sceptical about these things, I'm not so sure how much value they have – if they are offering rewards, why not use them? Take advantage of them, if you can read the small print and work out exactly how "rewarding" they are. This is where some knowledge is good to have as it can be confusing to some if you don't understand the finer points of "bank-speak".

8. Be very aware of cashback for hidden charges that maybe on the account. If you want to use credit cards, because some people do use them for transferring, some cards like MBNA and others will allow you to transfer a credit balance in cash into your bank account, so there are those that advise using that sort of finance for even property purchase and that can be only in a situation whereby the property can be refinanced and the money taken out and repaid back to the credit card. So again, be careful with that but it is a useful facility if you needed cash quickly. Interest rates are going to be high, but it's there, it's a source.

You don't have to grovel for it if the account is set up that way – you can take advantage of it if you wish.

9. And so you can play these systems to gradually increase your credit and you can make transfers from one account to another, as you know, you can transfer balances and they say there's no interest on the balance transfer, but they charge you a 3% fee for it. Well, with money it's only basically a base rate of half of one percent. The London inter-bank rate is, whatever it is it's going to be varying, let's say it's 1.5-2%, they're actually charging you a fee of 3% which can only be for a period of six months so that's actually 6% per annum, so they're actually still making quite good money out of you that way.

10. And finally, with the Credit Card 10 Commandments – pay off your monthly balance unless you've really got problems, always pay it off because that is the cheapest way and the most direct way of saving money by paying off credit cards, because as we have said ad nauseum so far in this book, and website, you're not going to get much money from your investments.

So, let's move on. We're still in defensive mode, and this is a little section I like to call 'Beat The Banks'.

BEAT THE BANKS

I believe in "playing the game" and have some great methods for "beating the banks." No one likes being ripped off by financial institutions, we know that the banks are out there essentially to make as much money as they can out of us. We know that bankers are programmed to do that, even the high street banks, and of course we are bombarded with massive amounts of publicity saying what good guys they are and how they are doing everything in our interest and so forth, but, well… hmmm… we know differently.

So, playing them at their own game is something we know all about. It's not about breaking any rules or laws, rather playing the system to take advantage of it because believe you me, the system is there for you to use… rather than be abused by it.

THE UK IS VERY COMPETITIVE

There's a lot of banks out there, they've had all sorts of problems, but they are pretty competitive and again, it's all about making the most of new deals and offers and better interest rates and less fees. The banks were lucky I think to get away with the massive bail-out at our expense a few years ago, at the taxpayer's expense, and what do we get from the bail-out? Nothing really that I can see. But there are at least some small ways we can something back from them. Not letting them take our money unnecessarily is one way of doing this, as you'll see…

AVOID OVERDRAFTS

Avoid overdrafts unless you really need them. I'm stating this again, but this is painfully obvious and very simple stuff. Overdrafts can whittle away at your bank account and very quickly plunge you into debt. Not big debt, but it's still money you are LOSING, not saving. Why let your money disappear unnecessarily simply because you keep slipping into overdraft? It doesn't make sense really, does it? It might only be a few quid a month – but it's still a few quid that could have been going elsewhere – i.e. into a savings fund!

MOST FEES ARE NEGOTIABLE

Once again – if you don't ask, you won't get. If you don't ask, you will never know. Never assume everything is set in concrete. The bank may say to you, "Well, no, we can't reduce that fee on this account, but would you like another account we have that has reduced fees?" Or words to that effect. Negotiate, it's often worth the effort. Seem like too much hassle? Well, it's not really. If you change your mind-set. Think of it as a profit-making endeavour, that you may end up saving a few valuable pounds each month. What will that take? Thirty minutes at most? The best part it – it leaves you feeling good after a successful negotiation!

ONLINE

Obviously start using online banking, it's a great feature these days, especially for keeping on top of your finances. But it is also excellent for anyone in business for obvious reasons. I think I started online banking around the year 2000 when Lloyds first launched it and it was wonderful and that was 18 years ago. It's great. I mean back in the day you had to phone up to do your banking and make transactions, now it is much, much better, making bank transfers quicker and money coming in clears instantly in most cases.

INTEREST RATE ON CREDIT BALANCES

See if you can get an account, and Martin Lewis the Money Expert can help with this, an account where you get interest payment on credit balances, even if it's only a small one. Try and get that, it's an additional benefit. There are many accounts out there that offer this, in fact there is an on-going glut of them really. But they can be advantageous, so it's well worth shopping around.

BEWARE OF "BENEFITS"

It may seem attractive and enticing to go for some deals the high street banks offer, but what looks good doesn't necessarily mean it is going to be cost-saving. For instance, I recently signed up for an all-round insurance package with Lloyds Bank paying something like £22-£25 a month for mobile phone insurance, breakdown cover, travel insurance, and a few other things. However, it is quite possible I may in fact be paying a tad too much compared to taking out these insurances separately. The advantage of course, is that they're all under one umbrella policy which is actually really convenient. But am I saving any money? Possibly not. So always check as all that glitters is not always gold.

SEPARATE SAVINGS ACCOUNT

Always keep separate savings accounts, and actually I am a great believer in multiple bank accounts and preferably bank accounts in different countries. We're not talking about tax evasion here, simply that it is useful to spread your wealth in this way.

DON'T PUT "ALL YOUR EGGS IN ONE BASKET"

I don't like banks to have it all, I don't like to put all my eggs in one basket. I don't like letting them know everything that is going on because they have got no right to know that and they don't need to know that. So why let them know? They want to know everything about us, but of course do we know much about them? Do we know that Northern Rock in the autumn of 2007 was going to go bust? Did we know that the whole banking system was about to collapse because of profligate spending on their part and lack of control? No. And yet they want to know everything about us. So don't put all your eggs in one basket.

PRIVATE BANKING

It's well worth having a look at private banking. Private banking has come on a lot in recent years, it is now available, like our theme tune, for the many not just the few. Private banking has become more accessible to different levels of income. You don't have to be a multi-millionaire to have private banking these days, although if you are, it helps.

They're not too keen on people with property assets, they really want people with investment funds is the term. And they're also looking for high net-worth individuals, of which there are lots around these days, and I'm sure for those of you reading this book, if you follow these instructions you will undoubtedly achieve, but banks, like for example the Metro bank, they're offering private banking and that's quite nice because you get away from the call centre so if you need to call you get a private banking manager, which is quite helpful.

Again, you may wonder if all this is worthwhile. Is there really any point to going to all this effort to save a few quid? Well, frankly, I say yes sir-ree! It is well worth it. Why? Because not only are you looking after your money more efficiently and keeping more of it rather than giving it to the banks unnecessarily – *beating the banks* gives you a great feeling of self-worth and sense of elation. Well, it does to me!

The "system" is there to be played. I play it, why not?

Another way to play and beat the system is a sort of reverse psychology thing.

PAY YOURSELF FIRST

Might seem obvious – as much of what I am telling you will! – but it actually makes sense. Think of yourself first before spending your money and giving it to the system. They can wait.

So one of the key things about defensive strategies is, and this came out in the famous book *The Richest Man in Babylon* by George S. Clason (and you will see this and others at the end of this book in our recommended reading list, books you really should get into) that you should pay yourself first that is the first thing. It's a strange concept, isn't it? Yeah, you should have your saving account or savings accounts, take that 10, 20, 30% that we talked about earlier outside of your 60% average running cost on a monthly basis, take that and stick it into an account. Pay yourself first.

And once that is out of the way and obviously you have paid your rent and your mortgage and your utilities, you will find a way of living on the rest. If you're living the other way around that 10, 20 or 30% that could be put aside will be frittered away. So love yourself, pay yourself first.

PENSIONS

Well we're going to talk about Pensions... not very exciting? Yes, you may think that, but sorry you are wrong, wrong, wrong!

Over the years they have got a really bad reputation, essentially because of the endowment scandal.

In the past Endowments were sold to provide pensions and the underlying assets performed badly, thus at retirement age... there was not enough money in the pot to provide a decent pension income.

(You can read articles on Endowment Mis-selling Compensation... and call the Financial Services Hotline on this topic 0800 111 6768)

However, the pension itself should not really be blamed for these difficulties, as the pension is nothing more than a tax saving investment funded partially by HMRC... what's not to like about that?

And it gets better if you have an occupational pension, your employer will be funding a chunk as well! So really you get a double whammy!

So I really like pensions, especially if you are under 40... Why? Because you get to use Einstein's favourite technique, no 6 in 7 Pillars of financial wisdom ... Compounding, along with No7, Pound Cost Averaging.

I don't think you rely just on a pension for retirement, but also have some property, maybe an ISA or two and other business and investments which we are highlighting in this book.

So with a pension you are effectively putting money away now for that future time, with contributions from you, your employer, and the government as well in terms of tax relief. (Remember, this is also a major item in the 7 pillars, taking advantage of government tax breaks!)

So if you're under 75 you are refunded the tax on all contributions, and capital gains on investments made through the pension are mostly tax free.

Also under the new law effective from the 2014 Budget, you can start accessing your pension pot after 55... (be careful with this... only take out funds for a solid investment or perhaps a life style choice e.g. a trip around the world.)

What should I save in a pension?

Start with your age at starting the pension, divide by two and put this percentage of your income before tax each month or year into a pension until retirement.

Example, you start at age 38, then put 19 % of your gross income in your pension.

So don't delay, the sooner you start the quicker you'll get the benefits, and don't worry if you feel you can"t afford that percentage, start with a lower amount and increase it every 6 months to a year.

With the range of pension products available now... it really is a no brainer!

How much can you put in? You can put in pretty much whatever you want, but there is indeed a limit on the amount of tax relief you can get... do check on line for latest tax reliefs and use the Money Advice Service's pension calculator.

So now let's look at the bewildering array of Pension Products out there, and I'm not going to give too much detail to try to keep things straightforward:

Company Pension or Workplace Pension

This is simply a scheme set up and managed by your employer to which you contribute and to which your employer normally will match your contribution. Speak to your employers and their fund manager (often an external fund manager or IFA) and find out what's being invested in and what returns they have experienced over the last few year. If returns are good i.e. 8% or more per annum, maybe you'd like to top up your investments with them? These schemes can be referred to as Money Purchase Pension Plan or a Defined Contribution Plan.

Also Additional Voluntary Contributions (AVC's) can be made on these pensions to boost your pension.

Auto Enrolment

From 2018, by law, employers will have to contribute to your pension, and set up a company pension. You will be automatically enrolled in this unless you "opt out". Again check the investment, don't be passive, find out what the returns are, and if they are dismal then you don't have to continue… but remember the employer is likely to be doubling your own contribution!

Final Salary Scheme

Back in the day, most company schemes were of this sort and it simply means that your pension payment is based on what your final salary is when you retire... so really golden handcuffs if you are earning well. This kind of scheme is less common today.

Private or Personal Pensions

This is where you, not your employer arrange the pension and pay the contributions without any contribution from employer. (Unless you can negotiate or they are willing to contribute.)

One benefit that I see here is that you can continue contributing your whole life and it is under your control, and contributions will not stop if you leave that particular employ. They started becoming popular in the 1980s and continue to be so, I like them.

You get the same tax benefits, and you can take a tax free cash lump sum from the pot and use the balance to buy an Annuity, which will give you a guaranteed life income for investing the lump sum.

Alternatively you leave the funds in place and take an income from the fund...or finally withdraw the whole lot (but pay tax on it... ouch!) And finally be very, very, very careful of the provider's fees... many brokers and providers have got fat on charging you fees whilst your pot loses value, and fees are major factor in reducing the returns that your pot will generate... so remember check the fees!

Unless you are super confident in your choice, I would recommend using a good Independent Financial Advisor (IFA), someone you feel you can trust and you have certain chemistry with, and preferably someone local to you, who maybe has been recommended. Better to pay something for advice now, rather than lose thousands over the years.

These sites may help you to find the right individual:

www.unbiased.co.uk

www.vouchedfor.co.uk

Self Invested Personal Pension (SIPP)

Just another sort of personal pension... you can dictate what your funds are invested in ..and you get the tax relief.

Small Self – Administered Scheme (SSAS)

Typically only available for directors of a business, not employees (another reason for starting your business?). They are quite complex and restricted to 11 members. You may invest in certain classes of commercial property.

Stakeholder Pensions

Once again, another personal pension, but with much more government rules and administration, re access, management charges, and terms to ensure they offer security and value for money.

The schemes must be run by an authorised stakeholder manager or trustee to ensure all legalities are met. The schemes are very flexible and you can start paying as little £25 contribution, and stop and start payments with no penalties.

State Pension (Old Age Pension)

This is what your national insurance contributions are for ...and to get the full pension you need to have contributed more than 30 years. That's a long time. However more than half the working population in the UK has no other pension provision so this one is important!

Don't let yourself be one of the millions solely dependent on this pension! Check your pension entitlement today at www.yourpension.gov.uk!

What happens when I retire?

There are many options open to you on retirement for you to explore, and again, this is not intended as an exhaustive guide to pensions, just a gentle prod TO MAKE SURE YOU GET ONE! You'll be amazed… the years can fly by, and nothing frustrates me more than younger folk ignoring the whole subject and saying, "I'll deal with that later." Deal with it TODAY!

RESOURCES

- *How To Manage Your Credit Card Debt:* Petreen R Mathews
- *How to Survive And Succeed Without a Credit Card*: Bert A Berthelsen

- *How To Manage And Conquer Credit Card Debt*: William N Woodward
- *Brilliant Budgets & Despicable Debt*: Heidi Farrelly
- *Beat The Banks*: Jasmine Birtles
- *Finance: Beat The Banks & Make Money*: Carl D Nuttall
- *DIY Pensions - A Simple Guide*: John Edwards
- *FT Guide To Saving & Investment For Retirement*: Yoram Lustig

CHAPTER 7

The WHOLISTIC Approach

Okay, now before we move away from the defensive strategies, a word about our general approach with *The Wealth Tree*. Again, this I have tested on numerous occasions with private mentoring clients and I find it's a very, very popular concept. The clients may be people who have managed to accumulate some assets, some wealth, and they can also be people who are really not wealthy at all but are working hard in some very basic jobs, so I have worked with many people across different groups and I wouldn't say they are completely "high net-worth" individuals but certainly I'm thinking of some clients who are really quite well established and who want to make a change in their life. Whether you are at the very beginning of the pay scale or the very top, there is always scope for improvement – and again, that is what we are aiming for with this book and our website.

As I mentioned earlier, I like to adopt a "wholistic" approach.

We will be looking at **Diet** and we are going to focus on that just a little. Are you eating well? You know the sorts of things you should be eating (you shouldn't be eating kebabs and too many pizzas). You need a balanced diet of protein, a lot of fruit and vegetables. Why? Because nutritious foods help keep the mind clear and open and that in turn improves our ability to focus and have the clean energy we need to drive on and make good decisions.

So, yes, you want to be careful about alcohol intake and obviously not doing drugs and not smoking. "You are what you eat." It's an old saying, but like many old sayings it is true! And you'll especially notice that someone of my generation, when you get to be a little older like me, you can actually see it in people's faces and I can look at people and pretty much tell if they have been drinking whisky for some time or abusing themselves in some way. I find it sad actually, when I see people who have wasted their health away or are actually doing it. I think to myself, *Why? Why do that to yourself?* I guess there is a lot of truth to the other saying, that you should love yourself first. When you can do that, you are in a better pace to love others.

And of course your **Weight** is important, you need to try to be operating at a reasonable weight, so keep fit, keep active. I personally don't think you need to go to a gym, but you do need to keep fit and active. Exercise is very important. It prevents lethargy and like nutritious food, exercise, expending energy, helps you to feel re-energised and ready to go! They say any movement is good, so if you're sitting at a desk all day or have some other stationary activity, just remember to stretch your legs and arms, get up from the desk and stretch. All movement helps the blood flow and feed the brain. It's shaking the cobwebs free every half hour or so.

And walking is good. Instead of driving to work or even getting public transport – why not walk it, if it is within reasonable distance of course? Or when you go shopping. Why take the car if you don't really need to? Walking is good.

And of course you need to be feeding your **Mind**, the mind that is going to help you set about getting yourself off your knees (if you are on your knees), to be standing. If you're already standing, we want to get you from standing to starting to walk towards your goals of attaining financial freedom. If you are already walking towards your goals, we want to be able to get you jogging then running towards them. So whatever stage you're at, you need *health*. You need *fitness*. Trying to do good business or a good job, if you're not in good shape, it's tough and it will lead to a lack of energy, it will lead to being a couch potato, and it won't help you towards your goals.

So remember that. We are looking at the *wholistic* approach, we are looking at diet and exercise, to ensure that your mind is in good shape as part of your body and then of course feeding the mind, as we have already touched upon, with books, training and potentially mentoring and having people around you who are stimulating and not dragging you down. It's all good stuff that will help you become a new YOU.

And that is essentially what we are talking about – creating a new mind-set for you in the way you approach your life and you wealth. It's all interlinked. It all counts. Part of the whole. When you start thinking like this, well, anything can happen. Anything good, that is.

JUST A FEW FURTHER THOUGHTS ON "HEALTH"

Firstly I would divide being healthy into two distinct areas. Unfortunately with these two areas, one of them does not seem to be recognised by the other.

Western health

This of course is going to the gym, being healthy, taking exercise, controlling your diet, and drinking in moderation (the World Health Organisation now says for men and women 14 units per week, that's basically an average glass of wine per day or a can of beer).

In the last 20 years there have been fantastic advances in understanding fitness and health. I would strongly recommend Dr Michael Mosley and his current TV programmes, many of which are ground breaking, for example his Fasting, and the HIIT exercise regime.

Regarding diet, of course I'm not going to dwell on this too much as there is ample material available on the market on the subjects but just to say I personally tend to eat a Mediterranean-type diet. We have, particularly in Spain, salad with most meals, eat a reasonable amount of fruit and whilst I personally don't feel it necessary to be vegetarian I have every respect and mostly I tend to eat a lot more fruit and vegetables than I do meat. Of course fish is excellent too.

I used to be a member of the Institute of Nutrition back in the days when there wasn't so much information available publicly but now it's pretty clear the kind of foods we should be eating.

Regarding all the diet fads out there, personally I have little time for this and I think there is a huge industry offering people all sorts of stuff to play with and pay with… The simple truth is that it's about a calorie deficit… You just need to eat well and make sure that the calorie input to your "machine" is less than the calorie output; in other words a calorie deficit… It's so easy.

I would also recommend a ***Fitbit*** or other wearables that can track, incredibly accurately these days, what you're consuming and what calories you are burning. However there are many free apps like the Fat Secret that are free and to download… You don't need to spend any money really to do this, just a bit of self-control.

Regarding alcohol, I enjoy a drink and I love a good quality red wine but I have to control myself because I could easily polish off a bottle, so I've had a bit of a struggle with that, and I put myself through a detox program to cleanse the system and basically stop drinking. In 2016 I went for two months without drinking anything and it felt good, but also having a nice glass of wine with friends and in good restaurants also feels very good!

Eastern health

Now we can get into a completely different thing which is barely recognised in the Western world and that is what I'm calling Eastern Health, but really it's the Traditional Chinese Medicine aspect of health. Since my 20s I studied martial arts and was drawn inexorably to Chinese systems, what is called the Internal Martial Arts, the best known being Tai Qi Quan (Tai Chi Chuan) and the other arts being Xing Yi, Ba Gua and Yi Quan… The latter being an art that I studied for over 30 years in China, the United States and in Europe. These arts are tremendous for attack and self-defence. In case you have an image of grannies in silk pyjamas doing slow movements in the park, yeah, that can be part of it, but we also use boxing gloves and punch bags.

However, I don't wish to go on about martial arts; although this has been my personal path it's the health aspect of these and the development of Qi or CHI which is the most important thing and this manifests itself in the health side as many, many systems of Chi Gong… i.e. the development and cultivation of your Chi.

I find it very sad that many Western doctors (and I have given training sessions to groups of medical staff) do not know anything, or very little in this area, even the distinguished Dr Michael Mosley.

Basically developing your Chi comes from our various exercises of which the martial arts are one group but with Chi Gong the main reason for doing the exercises is health… These exercises are nothing whatsoever like Western exercise, they consist typically of smooth rounded movements, drawing in the energy of the universe which we believe is all around you, in opening the body, to open the internal aspects of the body, your spine breathing deeply, allowing the Chi and oxygen to circulate around you.

The World Health Organisation recognises acupuncture which of course is the positioning of needles on various acupuncture points on the so-called meridian lines of the body. Chi Gong is very much part of this traditional Chinese medicine practice and without putting in needles or burning hot spots on the body. We open the body, we allow the energy to flow and this really has a profound impact on you.

This is not a book on Chi Gong but when we are considering health, wealth and happiness I could not avoid bringing this in... it is something essential.

I know it is recognised more in the Western world now than maybe 30 years ago (I was one of the first in London to start doing Tai Chi)... So hopefully again I can open a ***lightbulb*** with this.

You're missing something if you don't engage in Chi cultivation and there's quite a lot of schools and teachers around these day, and books, and YouTube is full of this stuff so please don't ignore it.

(Being a Western male, I believe the right path is to engage in both Eastern and Western practices so I like to exercise, I use weights in moderation, I occasionally go to a gym, and at the same time I practice Yi Quan and Chi Gong).

Okay. So, it's time to move on and away from the personal development section. You've had a taste of what you need to do to *keep* what you've got – I will now show you some ways to get yourself some more wealth which, as you know by now, I refer to as **Offensive.**

RESOURCES

- *The Root Of Chinese Qigong: Secrets Of Health, Longevity & Enlightenment*: Jwing Ming
- *Qigong For Health & Vitality*: Michael Tse
- *The Way Of Energy*: Master Lam Kam-Chuen
- *The Clever Guts Diet*: Dr Michael Mosley (Book & App)
- *Conversations With God*: Neale Donald Walsh
- *Just Such A Time – Reconnecting With Your God Given Purpose When Life Gets In The Way*: Lindsay Bruce

OFFENSIVE STRATEGIES

Strategies, it's the offensive side of our *Wealth Tree*, the branches of the tree. It's all about *creating more wealth.*

In *The Wealth Tree* we talk about the **Defensive Strategies** (protecting what you've got) and **Offensive Strategies** (to actually create more). So, I like to think of the defensive strategies as the roots of the wealth tree and the offensive strategies as the branches of the wealth tree.

CHAPTER 8

Offensive Strategies

"You are essentially who you create yourself to be and all that occurs in your life is the result of your own making."

– *Stephen Richards*

How do you make more money? Are you in a job? If you are in a job what can we do to get you to earn more? How can you please your employer so that they are prepared to pay you more? If you're not in a job but in business, what things can be done to improve it?

Obviously this is a deep, deep subject but the main aim is to give you some ideas, perhaps ignite some sparks, as that's the general idea. We're hoping to ignite some sparks so that you go away with ideas that you can take further forward on your journey to financial freedom.

SO, **OFFENSIVE STRATEGIES**
BASICALLY INCLUDES:-

- ✓ Job/Career (Chapter 9)
- ✓ Liquid investments, Stocks/Bonds/Cash Funds etc. (Chapter 10)
- ✓ Business (Chapter 11)
- ✓ Property (Chapter 12)
- ✓ Information & Intellectual Property (Chapter 13)
- ✓ Other Assets… Art, Wine etc. (Chapter 14)

How many branches do you want, or need?

Each solid branch of the Wealth Tree is a stream of income. You've got your base, your solid base, a solid oak tree that has strong roots. You've looked at your relationships. If you feel there is something wrong there, and it's quite sad, in my mentoring some of my students say they are really up for this and some of them have paid a lot of money into this training organisation, but at home they've got a partner who is negative about the whole thing. I think one should always be sceptical, but that is a bit different from just being negative.

So if there's negativity there, if those around you are not supporting you, that's very difficult and I had one lady last December who had a very difficult situation at home and I think she was heading for a divorce. I must say, the mentoring probably reinforced that, and personally I wouldn't go there, but it was quite clear she wanted to go one route and the partner was already dead set against it. I think embarking on this journey to an abundant and healthy life and wealth creation had created more tension in the relationship, and I think it would have ultimately led to a divorce.

To be honest, it shouldn't be a struggle. The whole point of embarking on this journey is to achieve happiness. If you are reading this and are in a relationship that questions your intentions in trying to achieve financial independence, well, I can only say you need to have a good airing of views and try to come to an amicable resolution. After all, this should benefit both partners in a relationship and your extended families (if you have them).

Beginning this journey requires a healthy start, so please do ensure you are in the right frame of mind to make the start. It is crucial to your success. If ever there was a time when compromise was required, this would be it. Everyone needs to be on board because you will need the support of your loved ones for this to work.

Okay… a bit of a sour note, but it's a salutary reminder that you have to take others into consideration as well as yourself. What you may believe to be right for you may not be someone else. Our actions impact on others and sometimes we don't pay enough attention to that. We might guess someone will be right behind us or stand side-by-side with us, but unless we ask them we will never know for sure.

In other words, discuss your plans with your loved ones or partner ahead of time before plunging straight in. Communication. Very important, especially if you are in a relationship where both partners might be affected.

Okay, now I've got that off my chest… Onwards we go!

CHAPTER 9

Job/Career

I wonder how many of you reading this book are actually in a job. My view about jobs is this – some people talk about J.O.B. (just over broke) because many people, and yours truly for sure, have been in a situation whereby they're earning lots of money, they're rising up in their professions, maybe as a lawyer, accountant, doctor, whatever, and they feel they have to have the trappings. So the houses get bigger, the cars get bigger, the suits get more expensive, and the holidays get more exotic, and so they start spending to the limit of their income. So, wealth is not being created and it is very easy for that to happen.

What we are talking about here is **creating wealth**, creating assets that will generate wealth and that could be property, art, wine, going up in value or indeed liquid investments (stocks, savings accounts), financial investments. So, jobs are great and at the early stages of one's career it's good to work with other people, I mean in my view I had a great experience working for a major multinational across three continents and five countries, and I wouldn't have been able to do that under my own steam at the time. I could now, but not then.

So, I am grateful for that and I enjoyed it and it gave me experiences, a slice of life in the way big multinational companies operate, that you won't find if you are working for yourself in a local business.

On the other hand, like Richard Branson, who started his independent entrepreneurial career when he was 16, he got started young and that's good as well.

There's benefits to both ways, but I would say as a job, my analysis is the following: if you are earning a high income and you love what you do, you're a top surgeon, you're earning a six-figure income, then why would you change that? But you may want to be an investor in businesses on the side and have other investments going on, which I'm sure such a person would have, hopefully. Though I have to say I have mentored doctors who don't, they are in the "keeping up with the Joneses" trap and spending in order to keep up appearances.

If you are in that position, if you've got a high income, a six-figure income, you love what you're doing, then I would say, why would you change that? However, many of my mentees are in this position, which is, they are earning good money, five to six figures, and that typically puts them in the top 1% or even a half or third of 1% of the UK's population, but they can't stand what they're doing. Stressed out, unhappy, not satisfied, don't see a future, maybe they're in their 30s, and maybe they've been passed over a bit, or maybe their career is meteoric, but you know in the major corporate world it is a pyramid – you go up, you keep moving, but the positions at the top are relatively few. So to get to the top, to get to the pinnacle, is not so easy. Your face has really got to fit and you've got to be a corporate person as well.

So if you're in that position, whereby you're earning lots of money but you don't like what you're doing, then you really do have to be looking at getting out, maybe taking redundancy, maybe reducing the number of hours that you're working, take a day or two out, work less if you can (if you're allowed to by the organisation). Some banks for example, I have a client who works for a major bank, they would allow you that. Or take a year's sabbatical if that is allowed and take that time to set up your businesses.

On the other side of the scale, if you're earning little money, if you're only earning £15,000 or 10-20 grand, which many people do, then there's no question about it, you need to be getting into some sort of business and getting started, especially if you don't like what you are doing. I mean working on a supermarket check-out for example, well, that's difficult, isn't it? So in that situation you really need to be focusing on 'how can I make this change?' and not, in my view, as some people do, start doing another job and then another job in the evening.

I have two ladies, two mentees, who are actually, each of them, doing three jobs. And the first job was a full-time job and one of them was crossing from East London to South-west London for a day job and then doing some canvassing in the evening, and then doing some other job as well, just to make ends meet, to pay school fees for their kids and so forth. Now that's what I call *hard graft*. What a lot of effort. Necessary of course for these two people, but boy, what a tough way to make a living.

And that's where I come in, because this is what I do, I help guide people away from work situations like that. And, not to be big headed about it, I am successful at doing this. I'm not a miracle worker or a saint or anything like that, but what I do helps and I love it, helping people get on their feet if they're down or helping them to move forward and further away from actually *working* without meaning or enthusiasm for a living.

It can be done. I am doing it. And so are my mentees. And yes, I am very pleased about that and okay, a little proud too.

So, you need to be really focusing on developing some assets and starting up a business, maybe even more than one.

Still on the job aspect and the different types of job situation, there is a fourth quadrant, as it were, that you might be in where you're not earning much money but you love what you're doing. Now I don't know what nurses earn these days but that could be a case.

You love being a nurse, you love serving your fellow man, you like helping people, helping to cure them, to make them better, but you're not earning much and there again, I wouldn't say give up that job if you love it because that could be your vocation, that could be your life's work and major contribution to society, but you need help in terms of developing financial security and independence. And once again, that can be done – if you know how.

NOW, IF YOU'RE IN A JOB, HOW DO YOU GET A RAISE?

We all want to get paid more, don't we? Some of you might be working in the National Health Service, or in fixed organisations, civil servants, and that's more difficult where it's really structured, but basically if you're in a private organisation, and even if you're not actually working for the state in one way or another, what you have to do is start acting and thinking like an entrepreneur. You start having to think and act as if you are a contractor in a job.

So, I believe, and I am an employer, and I was an employee years ago (not now, perish the thought!) I believe that years in the job counts for something these days but not so much. What really counts is *productivity*. How productive are you? So, thinking like an entrepreneur, you need to focus on adding value to the organisation. Focus on adding value to your employer. Focus on showing your immediate boss, employer that you are adding value and creating value and that you're thinking about that.

I believe years of service and experience, of course this is valuable, but gone are the days in my view, certainly in my businesses, you know I hate rewarding just because they've been sitting on the same flipping chair for a few years. That means nothing; people have been sitting on chairs and coming into offices, it's well known that people working in an office for 35-38 hours a week, they're probably only productive for about 30% of that time and that's probably being generous, it's maybe 20% of the time, and by the time they've come in and said, "Hello Daphne, did you see last night's episode of EastEnders?" made a cup of coffee and had a chat at the coffee machine, "Oh, hello Joey, how are you are you getting on all right?" Blah, blah, blah, not very productive.

So it's productivity that we're after and that's what you need to demonstrate to your employer. Make a note of all the contributions, all the benefits, all the improvements that you have made in your particular job and task. Make a list of them, send an email to your boss. Write him a letter, have a little meeting with him or her and chat through it and say, but don't ask for money, say this is what I am doing to improve this. And make sure they are aware of it. And then also, ask your immediate boss their opinion on how you can excel in what you are doing. Tell him or her that you don't like mediocrity, you don't want to be ticking over, you want to be going somewhere.

You've got a mission and your mission is to improve your life generally. And the job you are doing for this company, ABC Company, is really important to you and you want to make sure ABC Company is the best in the field, the best in the sector and your department, let's say planning or manufacturing, is tops. So ask your boss, "What do you think I can do to improve what I'm doing?" and follow that by meeting and feeding back to him. Check the competition. If you're working for Mercedes, check what Audi are doing. How do they do things? Is there something you can learn? Are there some improvements you can make and implement from the competition?

And then finally once you have demonstrated, over a period of months, to your boss that you are very serious and you have improved, that is the time to ask for a raise. And if you don't get it, well, that's when you need to start thinking maybe it's time to be moving on, but firstly you need to prove your worth.

So, that's all about getting a raise. Always be positive. Get involved in role-plays and videos. This is when you are going in for an interview and you're actually going for a new job, so obviously if you feel you have hit the glass ceiling, that there's no way forward, that you really aren't going to get the raise you want out of this particular company, then you need to be looking elsewhere.

GOING FOR A NEW JOB

When you're going for an interview, obviously be positive, relax, smile. Smiling is so important. Being relaxed, I know it's tough when you're going for an interview, it's quite difficult, but smiling and being friendly, physical contact, shaking hands, very important. Try not to have a sweaty palm. Body language, your dress and so forth, these things go without saying, but these things are very, very important. These days if you are a guy, a lot of people don't wear ties. Know the culture of the organisation you're in; if you're in doubt be more formal, if you're in doubt call the person Mr or Mrs, instead of John or Jane. They will allow you to sort of go backwards and not call them Mr or Mrs but instead by their first names, John or Jane, but don't assume that. Also in a sales environment, be very careful because people of the older generation can be offended if you're too informal too quickly. So be careful about that.

They are actually having to teach people, by the way, basic social skills like shaking hands and looking people in the eye, and how to meet people and say "hello", because there is a generation that's come up that is much more comfortable sending emails, playing with smartphones, flicking in and out of the Internet or whatever, and they've lost some of these social skills. This is a fact, it's being taught, stuff that was quite normal, quite basic in the past.

KNOW THE COMPANY

Prepare, know the company when you go for your interview, know the company very well and know the position as much as you can. That's what turns people on. If you can come in and you know the company or something about the position and can talk knowledgeably about the market sector, and the company, and the position, it's impressive, it shows you've done your homework and then you can then put on the table. Let's say you were working for Mercedes and you go for a job at Audi, you can say, "Well in Mercedes one of the things I have implemented there is XYZ and I think that is really good, do you think I can possibly implement that here?"

And they will be impressed because what they want is someone who is productive, someone who is going to come in and is really going to make a change. They don't want mediocrity these days. So study and prepare.

How can you help the company to achieve its goals? Talk in terms of, and it depends on what kind of job you are after, if it's manufacturing, fine, but if it is sales then talk in terms of the sales achievements you have made and what you would like to implement in that position. If it's finance, how can you help the company to improve shareholder value? That's very important in the corporate world, the shareholders, they're the owners of the company. How can you help to make that value greater?

The immediate boss you are going to be working for, how can you help him or her to achieve their goals? That will really turn them on. Wow. Some might be a bit threatened if they think you're too hot, you may be threatening, you may be after their job. Well, that's the corporate world in a way, isn't it? But basically, how can you help your boss to excel? That, well, that would turn me on. I had never heard anything like that when I was interviewing people, but now, I have heard that, and people have said to me, "I think I can do this, that and the other," and that is very, very impressive as an employer.

BE CONVINCING

- Always, as well, when going for a job interview try and have a competitive job offer, so once again you haven't got all your eggs in one basket. If you've got a real job offer, great, if you haven't then you might want to invent one so that they feel there is competition for your services out there. Obviously make sure the company you are doing the interview for is aware of your successes and let them have appropriate stories of what you have achieved.
- You need to know what your total package will be. Not just the salary, but the whole package because it may well be, especially in this entrepreneurial world, that there are share options and a lot of companies now, and companies I have invested in, are offering share options to their staff. The staff

get an average wage, not terribly high, which helps the company out because they are growing companies, but they have the right to shares and the strategy will be a major venture capital investment perhaps in the organisation, which will mean they can cash out their shares and do very well. The whole thing could be sold out or they might be floated on a stock exchange. Finally, just be very upfront and convince them that you will definitely exceed your goals.

RESOURCES

- *How To Get That Job, A Complete Guide To Getting Hired*: Malcolm Hornby
- *How To Negotiate Salary And Get Promoted*: Daffodil Kelly.

CHAPTER 10

Liquid Investments

We, of course, are not giving any financial advice and we are simply giving a personal opinion on instruments out there, which are…

Stocks and Shares

Bonds

Cash accounts

Contracts for Difference

Options

I personally feel investing in Liquid Assets or Instruments is essential for your wealth building and is something ignored or avoided by the vast majority of citizens in many countries including the UK (but not the USA!)

Folk are scared of the potential losses and don't understand how markets work, etc. I think they are correct to be scared, but perhaps that fear should be replaced by "caution", as should be the case with any kind of investment and business activity. However, ignoring it won't make it go away!

So, investing in a SIPP Pension (as discussed previously) using the 7 Pillars Of Financial Wisdom i.e. Compounding and Pound Cost Averaging, will bring safe and steady results when invested in the correct instruments (see Point 3 below)

Analysts state that over many years, stock markets have outperformed property in terms of value… so my belief is that you and I should have our cake and eat it… i.e. a sensible investment strategy in real estate AND liquid instruments!

THE GOLDEN RULES TO INVESTING

You need to be careful when you invest and make sure you take some basic steps:

1. The greater return, the greater the risk… so if you're new to this kind of investing start slowly!
2. Diversify! Invest in a basket of stocks or a tracker fund rather than all in one stock, i.e. lessen the risk.
3. High Five! Seasoned players will tell you to invest for the long term… five years or more. Warren Buffett (probably the wealthiest multi-billionaire investor ever) has invested long-term for 50 years and has recently won a bet against hedge fund managers by his long-term tracker strategies beating hedge funds over 10 years!
4. Keep an eye every quarter on your portfolio… work with a competent broker (see resources below) and don't be afraid to make changes where recommended.
5. Don't invest in the news… the whole market will be doing this and you'll probably be too late.
6. Don't forget cryptocurrencies (Bitcoin, Ethereum etc.) but be extremely cautious. Accounts can be hacked, however I believe they are the shape of the future and are not going to go away. The whole banking sector is going to be disrupted fully. I recently invested in Ethereum as advised by my son, Jan Godfrey, somewhat a specialist, and did

very well for six months, but the value has recently fallen off. So these would be long-term investments.

RESOURCES

Books

- *Stock Investing For Beginners* – John Roberts
- *The Intelligent Investor* – Benjamin Graham
- *Fast Track Forex – From Beginner To Professional* – Intelligent Forex Trading
- *Stock Market Trading For Beginners* – William Buffet
- *Day Trading – What The World's Best Traders Know That You Don't* – William Buffet
- *Crypto Currencies – An Essential Beginners Guide* – Herbert Jones

Television

Both Bloomberg and CNBC Business are available on cable channels (CNBC often free) and by streaming on line . I would recommend engaging with these to get a good idea whats happening in the markets

These sites give research on Companies and Investments:

ADVFN – Live news, lists of gaining and losing companies, company-by-company performance charts, news and discussion forums.

Hargreaves Lansdown*- Offers news, guides and tools - and you can download a free guide on how to select shares. You can also sign up to a free weekly share insight email.

Interactive Investor – Offers information, news and discussion forums.

Motley Fool – A wealth of company-by-company information including news, commentary and comparisons of fund performance.

Citywire – Features financial information on companies, and is also a news source. You can watch shares in a virtual portfolio if you sign up for an account.

Investor Magazines

Money Week

Investors Chronicle

UK Investor Magazine

City Wire

What Investment UK.

CHAPTER 11

Business

"We see men who have accumulated great fortunes, but we often recognize only their triumph, overlooking the temporary defeats which they had to surmount before "arriving."

– *Napoleon Hill*

SO YOU WANT TO START A BUSINESS? BUY ONE? OR DEVELOP THE ONE YOU HAVE?

Remember your goals will be to move step by step to:

- Be self-employed
- Manage your business
- Invest and own a business or more
- Move to create a franchise or license or list your business on a stock exchange

Where you are starting or want to start is up to how comfortable you feel on the above ladder.

However, I think there's a great deal of good news right now for anybody embarking on a career, already in a career, wanting to start a business, whether it's property related or any other kind of business.

Tomorrow, walk along the street. Ask someone for directions. Ask them, "Do you know where this or that is?" Invariably you'll a get a tremendous, very helpful response. Not always, you might pick the wrong person. But 9 out of 10 people and probably more will be delighted to show you where to go.

And if you ask them for something else, probably not money, but something like do they know where there's a garage, most people are willing to help. I believe essentially that providing we act in a righteous and ethical manner, and you have that faith, the universe is there to help but also the vast majority of human beings are there to help as well.

Now there are certain countries in certain parts of the world in very, very difficult financial straits where people are not going to react in such a positive way, extreme poverty and so forth. It breeds hatred and resentment and animosity and fear. It's a fight for survival for some, it really is. So in places experiencing social and economic difficulties like that, the "ambience", as it were, is not going to be right for new businesses or enterprises. Not to start off with. That takes the work of governments and local authorities and local chiefs, to get social regeneration off the ground – and then new business can step in and take over and continue that regeneration.

Business in general has altered radically over the past few years. I am of course talking about the digital age, the rise and rise and stay of the Internet era – free, abundant information, goodness me. You want to find out something about somebody or where something is or whatever information it may be, it is there literally at the click of a keyboard, press of a button.

From a business perspective, it's absolutely fantastic. In the past you had to go through books, newspapers, make expensive phone calls, wait days for people to get back to you with facts and figures or research material, documents, manuals, presentations, portfolios all of which is time being wasted while you wait. Now, well, crikey – it's all there, it's laid out before you. There is the thought of course that possibly there is too much information now, but that's down to us ourselves, isn't it? We can judge that and we can control it.

Mobile phones for example, I mean the stuff we've got on here, this Samsung S9, the iPhone's the same, it's wonderful stuff, you get your emails. I got this free from my mobile provider like many of you will have done, but when you think about it, what's in here would actually cost about £1 million 30 years ago, in the 1980s, when you consider all the data it can open up to you – things like video conferencing on Skype, the digital camera, and so on and so forth, all that we have here on apps, and there's so much of it that's it's pretty much free. Incredible.

So, don't just say, "Yeah, so what? I grew up in the Internet age. I'm in my twenties and I'm used to it…" be aware of just how immense the Internet is and all it can do for you and celebrate it and guess what – give thanks! The Internet is going to be your future in more ways than one and one of those ways, without question, can be your future in terms of helping you to establish your financial independence.

I am not joking.

BUSINESS & THE UK

The UK is considered, globally, one of the best places for business. Many large companies, Google, Microsoft, Unilever, Siemens and many, many others – these large international companies are focusing on the UK and have created incubator sites to encourage businesses. The UK is considered for a whole confluence of factors that are economic, mostly. In the north you can say that the economy is not yet recovered, but 100 miles around London the economy in the main has massively recovered, and around 150 miles around London there is absolutely no doubt about that.

London is unique and it spreads out through the rest of the country and globally. There's all sorts of government incentives and support; some of it is useful, some maybe not so useful. The banking situation is recovering, the economy is getting stronger, the financial situation is changing and thanks to technology again, more financing options are coming onto the table, things like crowdfunding; there's an exponential growth in wealth and development as a result of technology.

I recommend you read *Bold* by Peter H. Diamandis and Steven Kotler, published recently, which really highlights the exponential growth that is going on in society and how things are no longer linear. Back in the 19th century and early part of the 20th century, growth was going along and then in the early 20th century started to become exponential; technology was increasing, arms manufacturing was increasing tremendously, then the Second World War happened and other conflicts which kind of held things back.

But now with technology there's an exponential upward curve of change and development, and you need to be part of that exponential growth. And I want to stress this, this is really, really important – exponential growth, not just in the UK but in other economies, you can be part of it if you want to be, but you need to understand what is going on. Don't expect things to be the same as they were 20 years ago. In the next 20 years there's going to be massive growth. So, we're experiencing big, big changes.

There are now, as I said, multiple sources of financing cash; the property market is bullish once again (though I fear we do have rather short memories. Only nine years ago, a huge crash and there will probably be another crash at some stage, there always is) and the UK SME entrepreneur culture is strong. For the last 20-25 years government has recognised that it's the SMEs (the small and medium-sized enterprise) that is the sector that is in growth because they realise that big traditional industries are typically still getting bigger, but they're doing it with fewer people.

So in terms of employment it is the SME sector that is very important. The UK is leading the field in helping and developing there, not so in other countries like France and Spain, they still have laws and bureaucracy which I would say inhibits that. So you're in the right place here, in the UK, if you are reading this here. If you're reading it elsewhere, these principles that we are talking about are really global but in this instance I am talking about the United Kingdom.

Another change in this exponential growth is the growth in investors. The banks for the last six years have been offering derisory returns on investments for those people who are putting money into banks. The stock markets are being positive and growing, but there is a big culture here in the UK of investing, and investing in businesses.

And that's been helped socially, I believe, by programmes like The Apprentice (not so much) but very much Dragons Den which was started in 2005. I think it's wonderful and I celebrate it so much. I haven't actually watched it for years now because individual businesses don't particularly interest me that much, but I love the whole concept of getting budding entrepreneurs in front of seasoned investors to see if the guys with the money will become Angel Investors for the aspiring wealth creator.

This is good because it helped make Angel Investors come more into the public eye and now there are many Angel Investor networks out there, so if you've got good ideas and they're in pretty advanced development stage, you will have a good chance of finding finance to take it to the next level. And if you are in property the same thing pertains. There will be investors for your business.

So, that's further good news.

STARTING A BUSINESS

There has never been a better time to start a business. Over 500,000 new SMEs in the last five years. That beats anywhere in the European Union and I think beats anywhere in the world which comes back to what I was saying earlier in this book, that the UK is a hotbed of entrepreneurial activity right now. It is a fact that the UK is considered the best destination, not just by us living here, but this confluence, which I touched on before, of factors. It's something historical. I believe the tax regime in the UK is favourable, maybe not as favourable for corporations like Ireland and other spots around the world, for a major developed country it's favourable.

The legal regime for companies is also quite favourable compared to some countries, for example in Spain right now languishing in jails, are various top directors of companies who have been convicted of fraud and managing directors and chairmen of banks.

In the United States, there are quite a few corporate execs in jail. I have never heard of that here in the UK. There may be, I'm sure somebody could tell me, it's just not something you hear of here. That's not to say that bad things are done here and people get away with it, just that it's a more relaxed corporate environment legally, structurally.

It's English-speaking, obviously, so we can take the best of what is coming out of the United States; the United States is synonymous with "pioneering" and more often than not is the place where many social innovations begin. The USA generates a lot of new things, but these American companies, from my own personal experience, and previous experiences, use the UK as a springboard into other parts of the world, most notably Europe. Often their headquarters for Europe, Middle East and Africa are often based here in the UK. It's a centre, the Americans love it, the tax regime attractive, funding is attractive from the UK, and London is a major world financial centre, as you know.

Without being political and I'm not expressing an opinion, just saying that what has happened in the last five years, the coalition with the Liberal Democrats and the Conservative Party, and even before that with Tony Blair and New Labour, they were very much in favour of finance and business and the whole City situation that allowed the crash of 2008, happened under a Labour government, did it not?

So Labour, Lib Dem/Conservative are in favour of business and there's some strange anomalies that have come out recently with the withdrawal of tax relief for buy-to-let investments and other anomalies, but essentially they are in favour of business.

Not expressing an opinion one way or another, I'm just saying that's the way it is, that all these factors have come together to make the UK positive for business right now.

I have already touched on the Internet, and in my view we should not underplay that, it's a huge advance, and exponential growth is coming from that and it means that instead of taking days to research a business, as it would have done two decades or so ago, it can now be done in just a few hours. More and more information is coming online which is fantastic and that includes more sources of funding. Crowdfunding is a major change. Lots of small investors are putting in money to invest in businesses.

> SO, WHAT DO YOU DO TO GET
>
> A BUSINESS OFF THE GROUND?
>
> HOW DO YOU GO ABOUT IT?
>
> DO YOU START ONE?
>
> OR DO YOU BUY ONE?

If you are going to start one, a good way to start is to think about your passion. What is your hobby? Is it something you can monetise?

A client who is passionate about exercising has started a business about exercise and diet for overweight women. So far it is successful. Many people are doing that. A hairdresser, someone who I mentor, has created a special environment for children's hairdressing and that is successful. Children consider going to the dentist and the hairdresser about the same, especially boys, and she's done that, she's taken something she's passionate about and monetised it and created a business around that. It's great and more often than not it is the best way to go about it because it means you are doing two things:

1. Utilising the knowledge you have in a certain field
2. Putting in the energy to develop it because you are passionate about it

And they say, the research is, that people who start a business around something they are really good at and passionate about, the two may not be the same of course, you may be not very passionate about it but you might be very good at it, they are the businesses that typically succeed. A lot of businesses are started and a lot of them fail as well, it's a fact that as Theresa May has said, they have created in the last five years, along with the 500,000 SME business start-ups, more job positions than the whole of the European Union together, here in the UK.

So, back to your business.

IF YOU DON'T HAVE A HOBBY OR INTEREST THAT YOU CAN MONETISE WHAT ELSE CAN YOU DO?

WHAT KIND OF BUSINESSES CAN YOU GO FOR?

There are **franchises**. You can look on businessforsale.com and various other sites like that. Businessforsale.com has been around for a long, long time. I sold a business through it in 2001. It's been around a long time, one of the earliest advice sites on the online market.

There are pure Internet businesses, a lot of people doing stuff online now, selling stuff, different products that maybe you can't get so easily on the high street, or through a major shop or supermarket. I have a client who's been marketing and has been for a few years now, fairly intimate products for men (men's health, let's call it!) which the men are a bit too embarrassed to go and ask for in a chemist. They probably couldn't get them in a chemist in any case, they used to be made in the States and now they're made in China and he's doing very well online with that.

Another client has a food delivery business, a frozen food delivery business; basically frozen fish, prawns and so forth, products that you just can't get anywhere. That is doing well too. So there's lots of stuff going on, lots of people starting businesses, multi-level marketing. There is a business called Shopping Sherlock which I think is the world's first online multi-level marketing, it's digital, there's no hard product that you have to sell or move around, it's very good to use for holidays, for flights, for generally buying stuff and you get commissions when you buy through the site.

You can go to business brokers – you can just Google it and a list will come up – who deal with "distress" businesses, which is something we're involved in, and this is where, through special means you target businesses that may be experiencing operating difficulties, and who could therefore use some help.

It could be through investment, could be a merger, we do M and A (Merger and Acquisition) activity in the SME market, bringing businesses together to create value, possibly to float, possibly to sell on.

You can also go to insolvency practitioners to find businesses with problems; there's all sorts of ways it can be done and that's something we will be providing more information on in ***The Great Book of Wealth Secrets***.

So, I'd like you to take a moment out at the end of this chapter as there will be an exercise for you to do, and that is to choose three ideas for a new business, or if you're already in business right now, choose three ways to double or triple the size of that business. How can you preferably increase the turnover? How can you do more marketing? Some people are looking for loads of money to do that and yes, sometimes you can spend a huge amount. But assuming you don't have tons of money how can you do that cost-effectively? Again, thanks to the Internet there are various ways that can be done now.

So that's an exercise I'd like you to do; if you've got a business and you want to carry on with that business, then three ways to double or triple the size of it. If you haven't got a business then think of three business ideas. Write them out and then talk to at least one business advisor, not necessarily with family or friends. However, if you've got a business-minded friend and your partner, your life-partner, then by all means bounce it around, but don't rush home and say, "Darling, I've had this wonderful idea, we're going to make millions out of this," because while they're feeding the children you could get short-thrift. So be careful, be cautious about how you deliver the ideas you may have. Take some time to think about it.

BUSINESS INVESTMENT

There are various sources of finance. Business Angels have been there for a long time. Again, we will give you resources of angel networks and angel websites and recommendations. Angelinvestornetwork.co.uk is one that immediately springs to mind which is quite a leading one.

Crowdfunding, banks, grants and loans, and of course, Mum and Dad's bank, friends and family. Certainly in the property sector, that goes down very well. Returns can be good, friends and family are often quite happy to lend, do a small deal to start with and then ramp it up if it's successful. Your immediate circles could well be appropriate.

Grants and loans, I have done a separate presentation of 100 different sources of finance. There are regional grants, there is support in multiple ways; it's just a bit mind-boggling really, it's a long presentation about as thick as a telephone directory. There is a lot out there, too much to go into at this stage. We will provide resources at the end of this chapter. But there's a lot of finance out there.

In terms of starting up a business, there's resources like startups.co.uk, Ten Steps To Starting A Business, a lot of online resources if you Google "wanting to start my own business", there's YouTube, there are business consultants who will help, but you don't need to do that.

I would stay clear of consultants as they are going to be taking your money and do not necessarily have the right information for you. But at this start-up stage you need consultants. Do your own research and by all means get in touch with us.

There are also trade shows and business shows you can visit which can prove very interesting and informative. The Business Start Up show at Excel in London is one example, but there are in fact dozens all year round.

So, in this book we're just touching on it, but again the idea is to create a spark, put a twinkle in your eye and make you think, *Mmm, that could work*. I was reading a book recently and I turned the page and read literally three lines, and immediately a lightbulb went on in my head. That's the effect we're after. Generating that flash of inspiration.

In this instance it was something that was in the back of my mind, something that was almost subconscious and I thought would be a good idea, and when I read this I was kind of empowered by just reading that half a paragraph and I said, "Hey, you could actually do this." It was about starting up a charitable foundation and I thought, *Whoah*, and then immediately I did some Google investigation and found out a lot more. But those three lines put the lightbulb on and that's what the intention of this book is, to get lightbulbs going on in your head. So that you can then, with our support and other support, go off and go forward and start moving towards building the business or businesses that you grab you.

M&A (MERGERS & ACQUISITIONS)

Yes, that's right, buying other companies! You thought that was only for the big boys? Venture Capitalists and the like?

You need to think again… because we are in the era of the "Demographic Cliff". Baby boomers who have successful businesses looking to sell, combined with the digital economy making communications quicker and easier, and a massive pool of investors with willing cash (after years of low bank interest rates).

There are leveraged strategies available now to buy companies in the SME market without going through the "pain" of creating one from scratch. And once you start, believe me, you'll start to enjoy seeing your wealth increase, and then really start to embrace the whole idea of financial independence. Trust me – it's a fabulous feeling.

EXERCISE: Take a sheet of paper and write out three ideas for starting a business.

If you already have a business: Take a sheet of paper and write out five ways to increase profitability, e.g. More sales calls/ Marketing… Price Increase… Costs Decrease etc.

RESOURCES – BUSINESS

NETWORKING EVENTS

1. Meetup.com

The daddy of event listing websites. This is a super-usable finder for offline events for just about anything – hobby, industry, stage of business. Search by topic or postcode, view other group members' profiles, create your own event and group, and do it all for free. Many meet-up groups also have mailing lists, which are very handy for regular emails and Q&As when you can't meet face-to-face.

2. Smarta

Well, they would say that. But they do have a thriving community of other business owners just like you, and you can help each other online (through our Q&A) and arrange to meet up offline. And, of course, it's all free.

3. 4Networking

We love 4Networking – founder Brad Burton is ace – and he's hell-bent on making sure his networking events are as unpretentious and un-pointless as possible. After introductions, you set up 10-minute appointments with the people at the event you think it'd be most useful to chat with. That means you don't waste time and you can achieve what you want to.

4Networking operates across the country and is only £10 per breakfast meeting – bargain.

4. LinkedIn

LinkedIn is loaded with professionals, and great for anything B2B because of that. You can search out people in your contacts' networks and ask for mutual contacts to introduce you. It lists events and has endless online groups where you can find like-minded business owners or industry bods to bounce ideas around with.

5. The Federation of Small Businesses (FSB)

The FSB is the biggest lobbying group for small businesses in the UK, and it helpfully organises local networking events that are well-attended by local small businesses. Each lists its own regional events. There will normally be three or four networking events a month, either free or roughly £30-45 for more formal golfing days and dinners.

6. British Chambers of Commerce (BCC)

Your local Chamber of Commerce runs networking groups for a mix of big and small businesses – perfect if you're after large contracts. Like the FSB, it offers plenty of free events alongside paid-for 'prestige events'. Dabble with the free ones first to see if the 'prestige' is worth the price-tag.

7. Business Link

Business Link has a basic search engine for its database of local business events, which spans free ones right up to those suspicious £500-a-day ones (we rarely recommend these, though some are occasionally good – use caution). The site is a little cumbersome but uses the enticingly labelled 'Method 2' to search rather than the altogether more mundanely titled 'Method 1' and your life will be much easier.

8. Findnetworkingevents.com

Does exactly what it says on the tin, for the whole of the UK. The events it lists are organised by various other networking organisations, so prices and format vary widely, but it's a good starting point for exploring what's on in your region.

9. Simply Networking

We love the fact that all of Simply Networking's events (which it organises itself) are only a tenner to attend. That's an absolute steal. And there are no sneaky registration fees. Expect 50-100 other business owners and professionals – a pretty decent number. Note: it only operates in the north of England.

10. The Institute Of Directors

Based in central London and various provincial towns, holds regular networking events and presentations, prestigious for meetings… well worth the membership fee!

11. <u>Facebook & Twitter</u>

Get a profile on Facebook & Twitter, follow people in your industry and you'll soon find plenty of good events dropped into daily conversations. You can also use their search to, er, search for relevant events, though this approach is likely to be a little more hit-and-miss.

Business Start-up Resources

https://www.startupdonut.co.uk/

https://startups.co.uk/

http://startupbritain.org/

Trade Shows

The Great British Business Show

Business Shows Group

Evenbrite.co.uk

The Business Start Up Show

The Business Show

UK Trade Show Calendar

Books

Crushing It – Gary Vaynerchuk

The Business Model Book – Dr Brock & Prof Gerard George

Entrepreneur Revolution – Daniel Priestley

Self Made - The Definitive Guide To Business Startup Success – Bianca Miller & Byron Cole

Business Magic: How to Buy Companies Using None Of Your Own Money – Guy Bartlett

Sources Of Angel Finance :

www.ukbaa.org.uk

www.angel.co/open-sourceincestors.com

www.corporatefinanceinstitute.com

Also, contact the author for more sources of business and development finance.

CHAPTER 12

Real Estate/Property

Another very important asset class is of course is ***real estate***. Did you know that the word 'real' denotes 'royal', and that underneath freeholds and leaseholds in the United Kingdom and several Commonwealth countries everything belongs to the Royals! This goes back at least to the Norman Conquest (please check history books).

But I'm not going to go too deep with this here because we will be writing about this in detail in a subsequent book.

Safe to say, real estate is an asset class along with liquid investments, business, intellectual property and so on. If you are interested in real estate, then you need to consider what sort of investment you're going to get involved with, mainly whether it's going to be a buy-to-let investment or full-scale new development or refurbishment.

Real estate has been around for a long, long time, since the Venetians, since the Romans, since the Greeks, Magna Carta, the Norman Conquest, the distribution of lands and estates by the Normans a thousand years ago.

Many of the noble families in the UK today are descendants from there. And it's quite remarkable how families and individuals can move from being criminal robber barons to being the nobility by sending children through the next generations to the right schools and universities and so forth. But I digress.

So, property has been around a long time, it's an asset class that right now, in 2018, the British are just so enamoured with. Martin Roberts, Homes Under The Hammer, I believe it's on five days a week on TV, something like that, and it's been on the TV for years.

And all these programmes about home and away and the country, in Spain or wherever, we just love it. It's an asset class that people are absolutely in love with. And you can understand why. It's very basic, even in this exponential digital age we're going through, the resources are there, it's much easier to acquire property than it used to be, with your Zooplas and Right Moves and your Googles and so forth, but there's more interest now, nine, ten short years after the crash of 2008, mortgages crashing, banks going bust. Only nine year ago, even less than that; some of the banks were still struggling four or five years ago. It's amazing, the short memories people have. And people are piling into property. But it's totally understandable. Property has always been a big draw for investment.

So let's break it down a little in stages, firstly between residential and commercial – close cousins, but with lots of differences:

RESIDENTIAL

BUY TO LET Investments

Put simply, buying a house for cash or mortgage and letting on a single contract to friends or family. Prices clearly vary enormously between the South East (London) and northern and Welsh areas. You are looking for a Gross Yield (Annual Rent divided by Purchase Price) of 7-10% and hopefully annual capital growth. Fairly straightforward, but beware of picking the wrong area or tenants, as it can turn into a nightmare.

HMO – Homes In Multiple Occupation

Dividing a residential house and renting by room… referred to by one eminent trainer as a cash machine! And yes, it is if done correctly. There is a lot of legislation around this and as of 1.10.2018 even more so, but it is a very profitable strategy, and one that we have used fully with HMOs in London and various selective cities.

FLIPS

Typically applied to distressed property where there is an opportunity to do a "make over" or serious upgrade of the property and make an interesting profit on the resale or continued rental.

AUCTION PURCHASE

Learn the tricks and tips to buy well and make a profit on the turn.

SOURCING STRATEGIES

How to find the best off-market deals out there… there's many ways, not just Rightmove and Zoopla.

LEASE OPTIONS

Leasing property (not buying it!) and renting it to a prospective buyer, making a regular monthly profit and finally a profit on sale.

LEASE TO RENT

Leasing residential property from an owner (again, not buying it) and renting it out to your tenants… again like lease options. An ideal strategy if you don't have the funds to invest.

SERVICED ACCOMMODATION

An interesting and growing sector offering holiday and corporate accommodation Check out channel manager www.EVIIVO.com to manage your bookings on multiple sites, not just Airbnb!

THE SOCIAL HOUSING MARKET

Investing in residential accommodation direct to housing benefit tenants (there are a few million claimants in UK), or leasing your house direct to a council or housing association for a fixed three to five year period and they look after management and light maintenance, and you sit back and receive guaranteed rent monthly!

BUYING ABROAD

There are spectacular gains (and losses!) to be made in the right area at the right time. The favourites of Brits and many nationalities are France and Spain. I have invested heavily in Spain and do developments there with selected partners. Buying for personal use or lifestyle is great, and the cherry on the cake is being able to rent it in holiday seasons. Check out www.fotocasa.es for Spain.

SPECIAL FINANCING TECHNIQUES

Learn how the pros finance their deals with Joint Venture finance, Bridging, Commercial and more… get other people's money to finance the deal!

So you have homes with multiple occupation, shared housing, you have buy-to-let investments, you have commercial investments, you have property development. I personally am involved in all of those. You have more exotic things like use of lease options and there's a lot there, and I can easily talk for hours on real estate.

Then of course there's foreign property investment. Right now, writing this, I am involved in Spain with a development in Valencia (which is a bit like Manchester), Spain's third largest city on the Mediterranean coast. Lovely place, charming old town; we're finishing the development in the old town and we're just about to start a new one converting an old mansion into ten luxury flats.

So yes, property. It's usually rewarding. But it's not something to be taken lightly. You need a bit of capital to start with, really. In all honesty, property investment is something you do once you have acquired some standing financially. You may need to borrow which is always a bit of a risk, but you will only really be able to raise any capital if you have some collateral, something the banks can secure their loan against.

Well, this is a huge subject indeed and obviously in this whole book, which I consider an introductory session to many of these issues we can only cover a small part, and I repeat what I said at the beginning. This is are not intended to be an in-depth training session or training manual as it were, in these areas, but it is intended to set off lightbulbs for further study and training.

Most people when they think of a property arm only think of houses and flats – they only think of residential, because that's what they are most used to dealing with. However, there is a huge and an arguably larger section in property and known as:

COMMERCIAL AND DEVELOPMENT

And this section is essentially split into the following:

1) RETAIL – shops and high street outlets divided between primary, secondary and tertiary areas. Primary areas are those where you are using all the big names in the UK: WHSmith, Costa Coffee, Lloyds Pharmacy, Boots chemist, the major banks and so on.

Secondary and tertiary gradually go down from that kind of quality to the lower areas, such as shops in small and back streets.

The retail market has of course been under attack for many years now by big shopping centres, echoing and mirroring what's been happening in the United States, and when big shopping centres take over they tend to not do any favours to the high street shops.

The local councils across the country and across Europe are attempting very, very hard to protect the high streets and to ensure that they prosper. This is a difficult task and in many areas it has been a losing battle, as can be seen by the number of charity shops.

However, coffee shops continue to sprout up along with beauty shops, nails etc., whilst clothing and shoes and agencies are disappearing fast!

Another factor affecting retail is of course the Internet and in the last 10 years this is taking increasing strides. You've only got to look at the massive Amazon distribution centres being set up, which of course are not employing many people because they're basically robotics. The delivery systems to your home are becoming increasingly sophisticated and same-day, next-day deliveries are becoming very common, so this is another threat to the high street retail sector. Unless you have massive retail experience, I would not recommend anyone to invest in this fast changing sector at the present time.

2) *INDUSTRIAL…* This category covers, basically, factories, distribution centres and any other place that is used for industrial purposes. These are connected now to the changing face of retail; the big Internet retailers are setting up huge distribution centres the length and breadth of the country in order to satisfy the customer demand.

Big retailers like Tesco and John Lewis and so on have had these centres for a long time and have been increasing them with the growth of the Internet. Many are being changed to robotics.

This, again, underlies the fact that the structure of industry and employment is changing exponentially, and robots are taking over in many areas.

So what in the Industrial Sector is interesting for the small investor?

There are opportunities to take over smaller units, perhaps, and divide them up into workshop spaces. We have done this in various locations; made the contracts 'easy in, easy out' with licences, without having to sign up to long leases, which by the way are called FRI leases (Full Repairing and Insuring), and they are often between 10 and 25 years.

3) *OFFICES…* Again, divided into primary, secondary and tertiary areas, the office market in for example in London and city centres in the city and the West End where rents are achieving well over £100 per square foot, is booming, with the new

towers – The Shard, "The Cheese Grater" in the city having been built in the last seven years after the 2008 crash.

However, the situation in secondary and tertiary areas is quite different as more people are working from home. More people are using the Internet to work, obviously, and can work from many different locations (including the beach!).

Many of these secondary and tertiary locations are no longer required and they are often above shops in high streets, and the current government has allowed Permitted Development of some of these units to turn them into residential accommodation.

The current Conservative government is focusing very strongly on allowing more building of residential accommodation and this conversion of offices is very much part of this.

This is indeed an interesting strategy for the smaller investor... so check out those unused offices, industrial or agricultural buildings to see if Permitted Development would be allowed. Check out the Government's Planning Portal *www.planningportal.co.uk*

4) *HOTELS...* Fairly self-explanatory, i.e. the large chains and smaller bed & breakfasts.

Many of the large hotels are franchised out from the main franchisor, for example many of the Holiday Inns are operated by different hotel groups under the main brand.

Again, an interesting area for the large investor; the hotel market is a thriving sector again with great changes, for example the developments in boutique hotels in the UK and abroad.

Smaller hotels may be of interest to the newer investor.

5) *OTHER…* This really is any other kind of building which doesn't fit in the above.

This could be a church hall, a school, an electricity pylon on a piece of land or any other kind of structure that you can think of falls into this category.

Some of them make excellent investments and are very interesting to invest in subject to who the tenants are.

6) *PROPERTY DEVELOPMENT*

Last but definitely not least is property development!

Obviously a complex area, however, I would encourage you, when you feel you are ready to explore some smaller developments e.g. *Permitted Developments*, building a house or more or small block of flats or a self-build. Again, when done correctly this is where potential big wealth sits.

Check out Self Build Magazine and the web and Plot Finder to find plots for sale… These references will lead you to more information too numerous to list here.

RESOURCES

Books

Successful Property Letting – David Lawrenson

Property Magic – Simon Zutshi

Property Investment and Development for Newcomers – John Howard

Property Investor Toolkit – Richard WJ Brown

Trade Shows

Landlord Investment Show UK

Property Investment Show

Real Estate & Property Events (Google this to find regional trade shows and events)

Training Courses

Rich Dad Education

Martin Roberts Making Money Through Property

"Yes" Networking Events

Trade Organisations

National Landlords Association

Residential Landlords Association

BPF – British Property Federation

Trade Press

Property Investor News

My Property Network

The Negotiator

Property Week

Estates Gazette

Property Wire

Property Industry Eye

CHAPTER 13

Information/Intellectual Property

An asset class that more people are turning to for income is that of intellectual property and information.

This asset class has always been there, it's always been possible to develop and monetise specialist information that other people seek and also to use the intellectual property that you've developed in a business or profession, again, is of interest socially or professionally to other people.

However, the big difference now is that whereas in the past the book had to be published and the publisher had to be convinced that it was worthwhile publishing, something very difficult for new authors, now self-publishing is so much easier and books can be published digitally, and promotion of such information can be done for little or no money over social media. The whole ball game has changed!

Now, the digital channels available from Facebook through Amazon and many, many more, make disseminating useful information so much easier. Webinars, video conferencing, Skype calls, gives every one of us a global reach to spread our message and the eBook and Kindle grow in importance every day.

- What information do you know?
- What information do you feel could be useful to others?
- Do you have a hobby?
- Do you have a pastime?
- Is it something that you been doing for years in your job, or professional career?
- Take a serious look at what information you know and you'll be surprised!
- It could be a hobby, crocheting, building children's houses; it could be specialist information on the Internet, it could be specialist

investment information in the certain sector of the markets.

- Think hard about writing an article and think how that could be publicised on social media on Facebook and LinkedIn, and possibly self-published and promoted through paid webinars.

RESOURCES

These resources are more than just monetising IP… it's a general tour of ways to make money on the web, but using some of these techniques you can put your own IP in some of them to gain a wide audience for your information. These tips courtesy of Digital Information World… Many thanks!

1. Affiliate Marketing (…and affiliate links)

An Affiliate link means you can promote another company's product and service on your site and when your visitors click through to the affiliate company and buy the item, you will get a cut! Commissions can be from 25% to 75% depending on the item… but you don't have to create the item, just do the front end marketing… it's like in the "old school" world, being a sales agent… Check out these sites to register as an affiliate!

- Commission junction – offers reliable products with on-time payments.

- ShareASale – mostly clothes, accessories, and other offline goods.
- Clickbank – high percentage payouts, but there's a lack of GOOD products to promote.

2. Pay Per Click Advertising (Google AdSense)

AdWords are the advertisements that show up on the top of Google search result pages.

AdSense is the reverse, allowing publishers (which includes bloggers and other website owners like yourself) to tap into Google's immense advertising network so that other advertisers can run ads on their website.

The best part about this system is how simple everything is.

Once you sign up, Google will place a simple code on your website that will identify the content of your site and start displaying relevant advertisements. For example, if your site is about pets (e.g. dogs and cats), Google AdSense will start showing your visitors ads for cat food, dog training and more.

You get paid each time someone clicks on the ad. (Yes, it's really that easy!)

Your cut might be anywhere from 50 pence to £10 per click. However, when your site has enough traffic, you can make hundreds (if not thousands of dollars) each month.

How to apply for Google AdSense?

- Apply for AdSense – Before applying, make sure you keep up with their latest Terms Of Service, though. Google has very strict rules, so it's hard to get (and stay) approved.

3. Sell Ad Space

The good thing about this approach is that if your site gets a ton of traffic from different sources, your simple banner ad pricing can go up to as high as £5,000 per month! However, the obvious downside is that if your site doesn't get a lot of traffic, you can't expect to earn as much either.

The other common method when selling ad space directly from your website is a simple ***direct price***. Here you simply name a price (based on what you think it's worth, relative to what the competition might be charging), and get paid upfront at the beginning of each month. This pricing is also generally a simple flat fee, not tied to a Cost Per Click like AdSense.

Where can I let others know that my website is selling ad space?

The most popular one.

- AdvertiseSpace – I haven't tried it, but it should be a good alternative.

4. Sell Your Own Digital Product (eBook, for example)

You have the potential to make the most money on a per sale basis when you can sell your own directly.

That's because there's no middle-man or person in between you and the buyer that's taking a 'cut' from the money earned.

This approach seems fairly straightforward because you can simply sell these products directly through your website and get paid immediately. Unfortunately, it's not that simple in reality.

Creating good products that are well made and polished require a ton of time and additional resources (like design, content, etc.). So there's a lot of 'hidden costs' in both time spent or contractors to collaborate with. Selling your own products on your site can also bring up problematic issues like payment gateways (how are you going to collect payment?), shipping (how are you going to mail or distribute the products?) and taxes (oh man, don't get me started).

And if that doesn't sound like enough work already, you'll also need a well-designed, persuasive landing page to make sure your product has a strong conversion rate.

ADDITIONAL RESOURCES:

How to sell products on your website.

How to set up a PayPal "Buy Now" button on WordPress

5. Accept donations from visitors

Don't have a ton of monthly visits, but you do have a strong, engaged community? Simply ask your readers to donate!

Accepting one-off donations isn't a fast road to wealth, however, it can help you cover expenses in the short-term if people like what you have to say and want to support your journey.

For example, PayPal offers little donation buttons that only take about ten minutes to add to your website, offering you a quick way to recoup what you might be spending on a good web hosting, new product creation, research, and all of the other costs to maintain a healthy, active blog.

For example, ***web.archive.org*** makes a lot of money from donations (most likely due to their ***millions*** of visitors per month).

How to set up donation buttons?

- How to take donations on your website – The right way.

6. Accept sponsored posts and articles

One of the common ways to making more money from your website means getting those visitor numbers UP. Once you've done the hard work of building steady traffic to your site with an engaged community, there are a few different ways to monetise your hard work.

For example, many companies go out of their way to look for blogs that will feature their sponsored content. 'Native advertising' like this works well because it still lines up with your site's primary content, so it comes across relevant and transparent.

You can also review the products from a company in an 'advertorial' that's part content, part advertisement. For example, if your website is all about the latest iOS games for iPhones and iPads, the creator of one of those ads would LOVE to have you review and feature their app to your fans.

When done right, this can create a win-win scenario. However done poorly, with irrelevant or inauthentic site content, and it can erode all of the reader's goodwill you've worked so hard to create in the first place.

For further reading:

- How to make money through sponsored posts and reviews – About.com

7. Generate 'leads' for other companies

Businesses thrive off new leads coming in their door to inquire about their products or services. It's no surprise then that they're ***always*** on the lookout, searching for creative ways to find new sources of leads to help them grow.

For example:

Let's say you have a website about teaching writing skills. Your reader's information (like their email address or phone number) would be of great value to different online schools who're looking to sell their courses to eager, proactive students.

Basically, you're connecting the dots; playing the matchmaker by introducing two parties who can benefit one another. While it's similar to how affiliate marketing works, in this case it doesn't actually matter if your reader ends up purchasing their product or not. They're just looking for an introduction at this point.

Where can I find such offers?

- MaxBounty
- Neverblue
- Peerfly

8. Build an 'Email List'

Spend any amount of time reading blog growth tips, and you're sure to come across people saying "***the money's in the list***".

They're referring to your email list, which comprises your most loyal readers. The objective is to convert as many strangers who visit your site for the first time into passionate followers who want to stay up-to-date on your latest work or content.

Admittedly this is a long-term strategy (and you definitely won't get rich overnight). But it's one of the best, long-term methods to profitably growing your blog into a fully-fledged, money-making enterprise.

Never lose sight of the importance in creating relationships with your followers, however. Offering great information or free help is a perfect way to start. Spamming people with unsolicited offers is one of the fastest ways to abuse readers' trust and sabotage your long-term goals.

How exactly does it EXACTLY work?

- Listbuilding 101 – Probably the best introduction on the internet.
- How to build a list with your website
- Best Email Marketing Services

9. Set up an e-commerce site (hard work is required)

Websites don't have to be just content. They can be centred around tools or products in an online store. Be forewarned, though:

There are literally hundreds of thousands of eCommerce websites or online stores. Make sure that yours is filling a unique niche, with a detailed strategy and the latest marketing techniques to stand out from the crowd.

How do I create a successful online store/shop?

- How to Make a WooCommerce Shop (WordPress)
- How to Make Shopify E-commerce Store (Shopify)

10. Flip Your Websites (Create -> Sell -> Reinvest)

Believe it or not, there's almost always a market out there for your website.

That means if you've built up a following (or possibly even sold a few products or included advertising on your site), you might be able to sell it to someone else and make a ***quick buck***.

To be honest, I typically don't suggest people plan on flipping their website or blog. (I'm a bigger fan of creating something for the long term.)

But you can't deny how lucrative it can be. For example, if your website is making £500 per month through selling ad space, you might be able to sell the site for £5,000 – £10,000 (which is about 1***2x – 22x monthly income***).

Another interesting option is to sell ready-made sites. These are MUCH cheaper, but there's still some money to be made.

Where can I sell my site?

- Flippa – The most popular website market.
- We Buy Websites – Another popular marketplace.

- FEinternational – Mostly for high-end websites.

11. Give away premium content for extra ££. If you are producing great content that visitors can't get enough of… you can always try asking them to pay for some of it!

I'm personally fine with paying for **premium content**. However, don't ask people to pay right away. Instead, stay focused on growing an audience and visitors first.

12. Start a private forum or coaching class(es) – Most of us have unique skills that others can benefit from. Setting up a simple forum or classes is an easy way to (a) help others and (b) generate recurring income at the same time.

13. Create a job board – Setting up a job board on your website is another simple, easy way to collect additional money when people accepting different job offers from various companies or individuals.

14. Offer consulting – Offering consulting gigs and providing services can help you bring in decent sums of money while other forms of 'passive' revenue take a little time to build up. You can offer these services via email, forum and or even Skype.

15. Add "hire me" page on your website – Your new website or blog is also a perfect place to feature your freelancing services. Showcasing samples or evidence of past work will help greatly increase your chances of getting hired.

16. Sell or rent internal pages – These aren't very common, however, you might be surprised at what people would be willing to rent or spend money on!

17. Display pop-up advertisements – Pop-ups can be extremely annoying. However, they're also another easy way to make ***some*** quick money.

18. Use content lockers – 'Content locking' is similar to hiding or protecting pieces of content until a visitor takes some action to redeem it. For example, maybe you want them to pay a small amount, or perhaps click on an advertisement.

19. Display audio ads – These are relatively new and are becoming increasingly more common. Personally, I haven't tried it. But I have read some articles and it definitely looks promising.

20. Sell an eBook – As already mentioned in (4) above. This one is a no-brainer. Many people sell eBooks through their site. **Some examples**: If you have a website about recipes and cooking, you can easily create and sell your own recipe book. The same applies in almost every single other niche.

21. Create a conference around your website – Lots of work, but a huge potential payoff as well.

22. Set up a teaching program – Kind of like a cross between selling your own content and offering consulting or services.

23. Host paid webinars – Similar to the last tip, which is largely a mix of consulting through content.

24. Create a membership site – Yet another tier on the 'info-business' model that has the added benefit of bringing in recurring revenue.

25. Offer coupons (with affiliate links) – People are eagerly looking for discount promo codes for everything from clothes to travel vacations. If you can (find and) offer a valid one, you can also get a cut of the revenue too.

26. Host polls on your website – Hard to believe, but easy to do!

27. Offer writing gigs – You can easily make £20 to £30 per 500-word article writing for other companies or individuals. There's also a huge potential for fluent speakers of different languages, as many companies want their websites translated by those who speak the native language.

28. Create a paid directory/business page – You charge people for listing or submissions to the page.

29. Just copy what others are doing – My personal favourite! 😉

And, once again, many thanks to Digital Information World!

CHAPTER 14

"Other Assets"

Apart from the asset classes mentioned above, there are more unusual or "exotic" asset classes like:

Art… Do you appreciate quality and buy well and allow for increase in value? Again, these days you don't have to spend millions at Christie's! You could consider investing in local artist's original work or those exhibiting in galleries. Do some research and get invited to artist showings… it's fun and you will certainly find work that is increasing in value.

A few years ago I bought a local artist's piece for about £60 and ten years later he invited me to his London exhibition where similar pieces were selling for £6,000!

Antiques… Ditto above. Can you spot a bargain in porcelain, furniture, etc. Quality antique furniture will appreciate in value, unlike IKEA!

My personal passion is quality Georgian or early Victorian furniture (they ain't making it anymore!) and chests of drawers, wardrobes, mirrors etc. will always increase in value. A bit like Georgian and Victorian houses.

Tip: don't buy in London… my favourite antiques emporium is in Ampthill Bedfordshire.

Wine… Do you like a quaff? Can you tell the good from the bad? London has many vaults and bonds housing millions of pounds of quality wines. I personally haven't invested in this asset class, as my predilection to consume would be too great!

However, my time in the drinks industry put me in contact with many professionals who could advise well on this.

Classic Motor Cars… Again, the classics in good condition can be worth a fortune; I have friends who invest here… not really my cup of tea, but they enjoy taking the cars out to Classic Rallies at places like

London's Hurlingham Club. So if you're a Petrol Head… this could be for you!

RESOURCES

Wine

https://apmwineinvestment.co.uk/wine-investment-landing

https://winefolly.com/tutorial/wine-investment-guide/

Antiques

https://www.telegraph.co.uk/finance/personalfinance/money-saving-tips/10115016/10-tips-for-making-money-from-antiques.html

https://www.muzeum.ca/blogs/news/12-tips-on-how-to-invest-in-antiques-like-a-pro

Art

https://www.cnbc.com/2017/11/03/looking-to-invest-in-art-how-to-get-into-a-millionaires-market.html

Cars

https://www.ft.com/content/fc2a08b8-f824-11e5-96db-fc683b5e52db

Books

Art as Investment – Robert L Lewis

How to Make Money Out Of Antiques – Judith Miller & Gray Jolliffe

Investing in Fine Wine – Alex Andrawes & Darren Scott

Investing in Classic Automobiles – Rush Richard H.

CHAPTER 15

7 Marks of Multi-Millionaires

"What we fear doing most is usually what we most need to do."

– Ralph Waldo Emerson

And it's very interesting, because we are fed, we are spoon-fed, by the media, all sorts of images about the fabulously wealthy, the superstars and entertainment celebrities and movie moguls.

We see David Beckham and his wife parading around in designer gear and going to restaurants and doing exotic things; it looks like they are being ostentatious and flash, but the reality is somewhat different. That is just the media exposure, it gives a false impression.

The thing is, you see, many millionaires would have built and considered the following to have been important:-

1) FINANCIAL FREEDOM AND FINANCIAL INDEPENDENCE IS MORE IMPORTANT THAN STATUS

This may surprise you, it did me when I first considered it; all the multi-millionaires, generally, over the years, through time, they mostly lead or led very frugal and humble lifestyles.

Don't believe me? Well, just consider this.

A row of terrace houses or detached homes, maybe somewhere resembling the place you reside. Now most of the people living in your street will be quite "normal", shall we say, not particularly rich or well-off – yet in the middle of your street or village or sprawling estate there will be a multi-millionaire living in there, quietly going about their business and life.

That's because often they are not very demonstrative. They don't like to demonstrate wealth openly. Why? Well, it's a combination of things, but mainly because they don't want to draw attention to themselves. And that is understandable really. If everyone knew you were a millionaire, well, you can guess what might happen next. At worst you would have a queue of neighbours all wanting to have a piece of you.

The celebrities of the world have no choice but to be open, after all, one feeds the other, so it's part of the media "game" (though privacy and security is a big issue, and that too is understandable of course).

As for the multi-millionaire living in your street – well, chances are they would quite possibly have last year's car and instead invest a chunk of money in a wealth-creating asset whatever that might be – property or financial investments or a nice picture that's going to appreciate in value. That's very, very important – asset-building. So basically, multi-millionaires typically live well below their means. I repeat, they live well below their means. Surprising? Yes and no. On the one hand, yes, you'd think they would be out there splashing the cash (and yes, some wayward ones do and end up blowing millions on a lifestyle that is chaotic and destructive – but these are usually the celebrities and movie stars and rock singers, etc.), but on the other hand they have learned about being frugal and building on the wealth they have created for themselves. These are the sensible ones.

Smart ones also know how to keep a low profile. You know this thing with cars, people want to demonstrate as soon as they have some money, or even if they don't have any money, they want a flash car because they just like it, driving around the streets showing off. It's status, isn't it?

But canny folk also know that the tax authorities, HMRC/IRS will also be looking at their car, will also be looking at their house. So you might protest and say, "Ah, no, I don't have much wealth," or you have it here and do your tax return correctly, but if you are driving around in a really expensive car and living in a mini mansion, the chances are they are not going to believe you and think you've got money salted away.

And this aspect of financial freedom is actually very important.

When we talk about multi-millionaires, back in the day it used to be millionaire, but now just having a house in London and you're virtually a millionaire, so for the ones who have more than £1 million, it's "multi". But it doesn't have to be multi-millionaires, what we're talking about is moving towards, step by step, very solidly but resolutely, ***creating more wealth,*** not having disposable income to fritter away thus leaving you with no wealth, which happens to a lot of people and I've said that so many times.

2) ALLOCATE RESOURCES EFFECTIVELY

So wealthy people, multi-millionaires, know how to allocate resources effectively to build wealth. The wealthy ensure their money works for them in business or investments.

I personally have had a tax, HMRC Inland Revenue investigation, and it went very well and they complimented me on how records were kept and so forth. I was told it was a random investigation, I don't know, so I've been through that route. So, you know, many people prefer to keep a low profile. They live well below their means.

3) THE WEALTHY LIVE WELL BELOW THEIR MEANS!

This in turn means they have excess money to use to increase their wealth. It makes sense really, doesn't it?

4) GOOD AT FINDING MARKETING OPPORTUNITIES

Wealthy people, therefore, multi-millionaires, you will find most are good at finding marketing opportunities to market goods and services. They may have help with this of course from someone they trust, advisors basically, but they will also, over time, accrue their own skills as an investor and spotter of potential.

You might call this work. But it's certainly not *hard* work. It isn't working hard for somebody else. You don't have to work hard to get wealthy. There are varying views on this, but I personally believe this: you don't have to work hard. Why would you want to if you didn't have to? Maybe if it's true vocational work you may find yourself working hard and living with the stress of that, but that's down to each individual. I think most of us, given the choice, would plump for a life free from the ardour of work that generally benefits someone else.

WHAT YOU HAVE TO DO IS

WORK SMART, NOT HARD

Don't work hard, necessarily. If you work smart and then work hard, then that's cool, you will get even bigger results. But so many people, and people I know, are working extremely hard and they're not getting the results because they're not necessarily working smart.

5) THE MULTI-MILLIONAIRE WILL CHOOSE THE RIGHT OCCUPATION AND BUSINESS TO GO FORWARD

If you want to be a municipal gardener you will earn a wage. It is unlikely you're going to get really wealthy working as a municipal gardener. You may love it, you may love working with the plants, planting out the gardens and the other council plots, but you're not going to get really wealthy doing that.

However, if you started up a garden centre and then opened up a chain of garden centres, you may get wealthy doing that. But you have got to understand marketing and you've got to choose the right root (excuse the pun!)

To state rather simply, *if you're working in Tesco's at the check-out, that's not going to work, is it? You are not going to go anywhere, long term.* So, choose the right route. And again that takes study and experience, support and maybe some mentoring, but get yourself into the right occupation or business. What is important is going with the rising tide. The guys who started the Innocent Smoothies brand, they started their business ten years ago at the start of an interest, more interest, in the smoothie market. People wanted bottled, pre-packaged smoothies like they'd make at home and they wanted to be able to buy it at lunchtime and take that instead. So the guys behind the Innocent brand started at the beginning.

The people who got into the mobile phone market 20 years ago, it was the beginning of the tide. Twenty years ago we got into the bottled mineral water market at the beginning; there was nobody else with the range of mineral waters that we had and there was a huge amount of interest in it and it took off like a rocket. Choose the right occupation/business at the right time.

What would that be right now?

I don't know; it could be any number of things that are taking off. Obviously Internet businesses 10-15 years ago, they were the way to go in a massive way, then the dot.com crash happened and then they picked themselves up and now they're flying again, so they are a must to put on your list of potential businesses to get into.

6) NOT INHERITED WEALTH

Typically the millionaire of today, the wealthy, financially independent person, will not have had "silver spoon" parents; 75% of the wealth created in the UK these days is self-generated wealth, only 25% of it is inherited. Now 30 years ago that would have been very different. Thirty years ago over 50% of wealthy folk in this country would have inherited it. It's very different now, it's much more self-starter, self-generated wealth through all the opportunities that are coming about through the changes in society.

Britain is less classist, less stratified in wealth these days, but it has become more of a meritocracy, a bit more like they say in the States and Australia. Well, having lived and worked in the States that is partly true, but there are still the upper classes in New England, the Old English as it were, though on the whole it is pretty much a classless system in the States in my view. Britain is certainly more egalitarian now, there is no question about that, absolutely no question. When I first started in business it was much more structured and the chief execs in major companies would often come from the best public schools and so on. That has definitely changed.

So, the entrepreneurs were hungry and they were hungry for success and most of them who have created the wealth have come up, many from nothing or you get someone like Trump whose father was actually a successful house-builder in Queens in New York, but he picked up where his father left off and developed it much more. As Malcolm Gladwell has said in his 'Outliers', if you come from that sort of background, Trump in that sense had a big helping hand to go forward didn't he? And some of us, like me, had no entrepreneurial background in family or friends at all, nothing. It all just came out in the genes.

7) KIDS OF THE WEALTHY

Finally, and interestingly, the kids of these multi-millionaires and wealthy people are very usually self-sufficient. They're typically not leeching onto their parents because the parents have passed down the ethic of work, of entrepreneurialism, and typically help the kids to go forward. They don't want to *support* them, they don't want to have people hanging on and just spending the inheritance. And on that point, by the way, statistics show that those that inherit wealth from the founder of the business or the founder of the wealth, second generation tend to fritter it and it's often gone by the third generation.

But there's ways around that, of course; starting up family trusts and family banks and so forth. But those are the stats. And the Rothschilds showed the way 200 years ago by setting up assets and wealth in different countries and sending various members of the family into different countries and different businesses to safeguard the wealth, as opposed to what happened with the Vanderbilt family in the United States; it was all inherited and they were immensely rich, this is in the 19th century, whereas the Rothschilds did this in the 18th century. The Vanderbilts now, I believe there are very few wealthy amongst them. They've got the name still but the wealth is all gone; it's been spent.

Okay, so they were just some indicators of the things you need to be considering and doing to generate that wealth and move towards it.

So, just to summarise what we have looked at so far with defensive and offensive strategies:

FOCUS ON THE DEFENSIVE THE "ROOTS OF THE TREE"

- ✓ The roots
- ✓ Control cost
- ✓ Plan
- ✓ Think of your banking
- ✓ Think of your credit cards

These Are Things You Can Start Tomorrow Morning

THINK OF OFFENSIVE THE "BRANCHES OF THE TREE"

- ✓ How can you start to generate more income
- ✓ From your job
- ✓ From your business
- ✓ Starting a business
- ✓ Think of your liquid investments
- ✓ Do you have a pension
- ✓ Do you have a share trading account
- ✓ Think about property
- ✓ Think about Information and Intellectual Property
- ✓ Think of "Other" Assets
- ✓ *Above all – take action!*

AN END TO THE BEGINNING OF

THE GREAT BOOK OF WEALTH SECRETS

"What holds most people back isn't the quality of their ideas, but their lack of faith in themselves. You have to live your life as if you are already where you want to be."

– *Russell Simmons*

Having ideas. It's wonderful. It's creative. From ideas spring just about everything. As I write this, I'm now looking at the inside of my house and I can see a sofa, I can see chairs and I can see the kitchen; all these things started with thought, man's thought. They were created. Everything we have on this planet was created in some way, by nature, by man, it's all creation.

And this is what you will be doing after reading ***The Great Book of Wealth Secrets*** –

creating your own new world, of happiness and abundance.

CHAPTER 16

Take Action!

YES, YOU'VE GOT TO GET GOING TODAY!

You have to get up off the sofa, start researching, start talking to people, start making calls, start sending emails, start getting in your car, on the train, on the bus, the plane, and taking action. That's why you need to be healthy, so that you can do what you need to do and do it in a relaxed and friendly manner. Don't tick off your partner or your wife, parents, whatever; there's no need for that because you're doing it in a loving way and I would strongly recommend you do it under the gaze of the universe, God, Allah, locking in a righteous manner; you should do things in an ethical manner to go forward.

There's no need to cheat. There are certain laws out there which may not be man's laws but they have been generated by whatever country you're in, invented by governments which may not be ethical in their own right. They've been created for whatever reason, so there are instances, I must say, when you may feel that a certain law is something that you are not too keen on, and I'm not advocating for one moment breaking any laws, I'm just saying that there are situations sometimes when ethically, you may diverge from what is actually on the statute books.

But generally, be ethical, righteous, loving, love and enjoy, give to the people around you. You'll find that if you give you get so much more back. If you want bananas in your life, go around giving out bananas.

If you feel detached, cold, unwanted, give love out and you'll get it back. People are desperate for that. Everybody wants it. Everybody wants love. The British are quite interesting, a bit like the Chinese, they have a slightly harder shell, have a reputation for being a bit cold and I say to people that is absolutely wrong; the British are very, very warm, but they have a bit of a glass case and sometimes that glass case needs to be broken.

In my experience, that's done very well. The more open and friendly you are, chatting to people, the more you will get back.

I'd just like to leave you with a bit of philosophy. From Aristotle Onassis, the Greek shipping magnate:

"It's during our darkest moments that we must focus and see the light."

So if you're having a dark moment now, in your life, if you're depressed, you think things are going really bad, it's at those times that we can focus and we can plan and see the light. And it's at those times as well the universe will step in to support you. Strangely, when we are at our most desperate, often this will happen. But you have to have that faith. If you don't have the faith you are denying the support, it's like being inside a cage and there's somebody outside who has the keys, and they can pass you the keys, or they can come and unlock, but unless you believe they're there and they say, "I've got the keys to unlock this cage for you, I've got the keys, I can give you the keys through the bars and you can undo them, or I'll undo them from the outside," then the door's never going to be open. So you do need to have that faith.

And that is something personal and something you have to meditate on. I always recommend people should go away and spend some time alone doing a bit of meditation. If the word 'meditation' freaks you out don't worry about it, spend some time thinking and relaxing, and focus on your past. As I've said earlier in this book, and now at this stage, you also need to focus on the universe, if you want to. If you choose not to, that's your choice, no problem, go forward under your own steam.

But I will say, if you look at the universe, my friends, you are a very little blip amongst seven billion on this planet. You are unique, you are special, but we have limits, we have intellectual limits. We may say, although that depends on you, we have spiritual limits, possibly. We certainly have physical limits; as an animal we're not terribly strong, are we? Compared to lions and others like elephants and bigger animals and so on. What's big is our brain and our intellect.

So I would say, in almost closing, why deny the support of the universe when it is there?

Some will say God, some will say Allah. I would say use that resource, it is there, it wants to help you. It wants to take you further forward. God in my view has no interest in you being impoverished and a pauper, or not necessarily a pauper, but living a life of want. It wants you to have abundance, because with abundance you will be able to help others in a loving way.

TAKE ACTION…

I hope that in the previous pages I've managed to spark curiosity and interest in some topics that perhaps you've not come across before (although nothing is new in the universe really) or topics that you were aware of, but haven't seen structured in this way. It's all about the various branches of the Wealth Tree, or generating different streams of income leading to financial security.

We mustn't forget, wealth is far from just money wealth; it's really having an abundance of character, having good health, good friends, good family, a good social life – essentially an enjoyable and fulfilling life contributing to others.

I believe this can be best achieved in connection with the universe. Many shrink from making the statement but I'm talking about God, Jehovah, Allah, a loving force there to help us.

I do not believe it wishes to control us in strict ways. I think it is there to help and I personally believe and have personally used this force to support me to move ethically forward in a loving way, and I would encourage all of you to engage with this force.

It's there to help us… why wouldn't you want to use it?

You may not believe, and that's fine as well, and I have no problem with that… but this is my personal belief and is shared by many.

Can you achieve massive wealth without a loving heart in connection with the universe?

I believe yes, you can, but I do not believe the ultimate spiritual and emotional wealth will come from that and I think ultimately it will lead to emotional bankruptcy and emotional destitution…

And is this really what we want in life? It's not what I've written this book for… It's been written to encourage you to go forward to grasp in a very, very, very fast-changing environment what's out there for you, but at the same time not trampling on others, but assisting others and of course looking after this planet.

I'm of the generation that did naturally recycle things. I didn't grow up used to being able to throw away televisions and electrical kit when they passed a certain point.

Televisions were a big capital expenditure, and were to be looked after and treasured and so other capital goods like furniture, and being in the property industry, we know we end up having to throw away a lot of the furniture which back in the day would be recycled. So I think recycling is absolutely essential .

As a sailor I see and I've seen on Atlantic beaches and in the Pacific stacks of plastic and actually, out in the open, stacks of plastic floating around, and I think personally, drinking out of plastic is convenient but the damage it is doing out there is terrible!

So I hope with this humble book, that I can encourage you to work with the universe, work with your fellow man.

The planet is growing to well over 9 billion people. Did you know, for example, that in 1960 not that long ago there were only 3 billion people on the planet?

Did you know that the number of motor vehicles on the planet has exponentially increased it is now 1.2 billion, and expected to grow to 2 billion (almost doubling in 15 years)?

I would encourage you to work with your fellow man; treat the people around you as your brothers and sisters. There's more and more of us with less resources, so we're gonna need each other!

If you do that you will you will get the benefit… You reap what you sow, you get back what you give out… If you give out unfriendliness and aggression and disdain that's exactly what you're going to get back!

One of my earlier Gurus, Sean De Warren, said, "If you want bananas give bananas, if you want love and attention that's what you give." So please, these are not my words, these are words echoing down from the ages. Look after your fellow man and woman.

In my mentoring capacity, my colleagues and I get to see many students who get fired up doing courses, get fired up doing a mentorship and then little by little without the support the enthusiasm and excitement wears off, and understandably they get sucked back into the daily life, to get sucked back into what they're currently doing. Many are not capable of going forward and creating the change they want and they seek so desperately.

So please don't be in that category. Don't go crazy; take things a step at a time. Analyse some of the information in this book, decide what strategy you go for, make sure that you are engaging in personal development, read books, attend courses, see stuff on

YouTube. A lot of it's free – you don't have to pay a fortune to plan your action.

GOALS… I haven't talked so far about goals. I'd recommend you set up your weekly, monthly, yearly, five-yearly goal plan and try and stick to it.

TIME… Set aside time to work on your new strategy.

PARTNER UP… Yup, and work with others and share. Don't try and do it all yourself!

GO FOR IT! AND IF YOU WANT TO CONTACT ME YOU CAN ALWAYS GET ME VIA SOCIAL MEDIA.

And thanks for taking the time and trouble to read this little book. I'm grateful.

A further quotation, from Steve Jobs to finish:

> *"Your work is going to fill a large part of your life and the only way to be truly satisfied is if you do what you believe is great work. And the only way to do great work is to love what you do. If you haven't found it yet, keep looking. Don't settle, as with all matters in life, you will know when you find it."*

ABOUT THE AUTHOR

Martin grew up in Fulham, West London, and after attending a local primary school went on to the London Oratory Grammar School, and from there went on to study law and finally qualify as an accountant.

He then went to work in the computer industry, working for two multinationals, based in five countries in three continents, gaining great international experience in marketing, finance, distribution, and how global players operate.

Always with a struggling entrepreneur inside waiting to get out, he went on to create three successful businesses and sell them before turning to serious property and business investment, in the UK and Spain.

Martin has been resident in Barcelona since 2001 and was recently remarried to Ana Munoz and has two children from first wife Teresa… Jan and Kristiana Godfrey.

Martin enjoys living in Spain with skiing in winter and the sea and diving in summer. He is a yacht master and has a classic sailing ketch, and has sailed the Atlantic more than once and spent several seasons recently sailing in the Caribbean.

Martin is passionate to help others move forward and improve their lives.

Do contact the author for more information, Wealth Coaching and other support from Martin and his close colleagues at www.TheWealthTree.com, and Thewealthtree@gmail.com.

Office: 0207 6177 898

15860862R00117

Printed in Great Britain
by Amazon